A SEASONAL GUIDE TO THE SHRUB & TREE GARDEN

Ann Bonar

Marshall Cavendish · London New York Sydney

Editor: David Joyce
Designer: Elizabeth Rose
Illustrator: Mike Bryan

Published by Marshall Cavendish Books Limited
58 Old Compton Street
LONDON W1V 5PA

© Marshall Cavendish Limited 1980
First printing 1980
Printed in Great Britain by Ambassador College Press
ISBN 0 85685 804 8 (hard-back)
     0 85685 808 0 (soft-back)

Contents

The Shrub & Tree Garden

Roses are the most popular and widely grown of all ornamental plants on account of their beautifully formed and fragrant flowers. But in addition to this major category, there are many shrubs and trees which provide long-term, trouble-free gardening for large and small gardens. Some are first-class flowering plants. Others have handsome foliage and among them a particularly useful group are those which are suitable for hedging. If you want a harvest as well as having small trees that are very decorative, there are fruit trees, such as apples and pears.

In growing any of these beautiful and useful plants, the golden rule is to garden according to season. A rigid monthly schedule fails to take account of the fact that weather and climate do not work according to such neat divisions. It is, after all, weather and climate which effectively signal the change of the seasons and which, more particularly, govern the growth and development of plants.

Weather and climate are, of course, not the only factors. The condition of the soil is also important. Very few gardens have the ideal soil, a humus-rich loam containing a well-balanced mixture of plant foods. But even though you do not start with the ideal, you can work towards it by adding compost and fertilizers. A regular supply of water is also a fundamental requirement for all plants. Going short of water means going short of food, too, so all the right fertilizers and manures will not help growth if there is not enough moisture.

Choosing the correct position for the plants you want to grow is also an important key to success. Planting according to particular requirements for sun and shade and degree of shelter, for instance, will give plants the chance they need to show their best. You should, of course, make sure that you start with strong and healthy plants, for these are much less likely to be seriously damaged by pests and diseases. Remember, too, that general garden hygiene, such as tidying up garden rubbish, will reduce the chance of pests and diseases getting a hold.

A Seasonal Guide to the Shrub and Tree Garden takes as its theme that the gardener's best wisdom is commonsense and an appreciation of the role of the weather. Each season begins with a summary of things to do which is followed by more detailed instructions on how to grow roses, shrubs and trees, including fruit trees. In addition, there are useful charts and a section on Controls and Treatments.

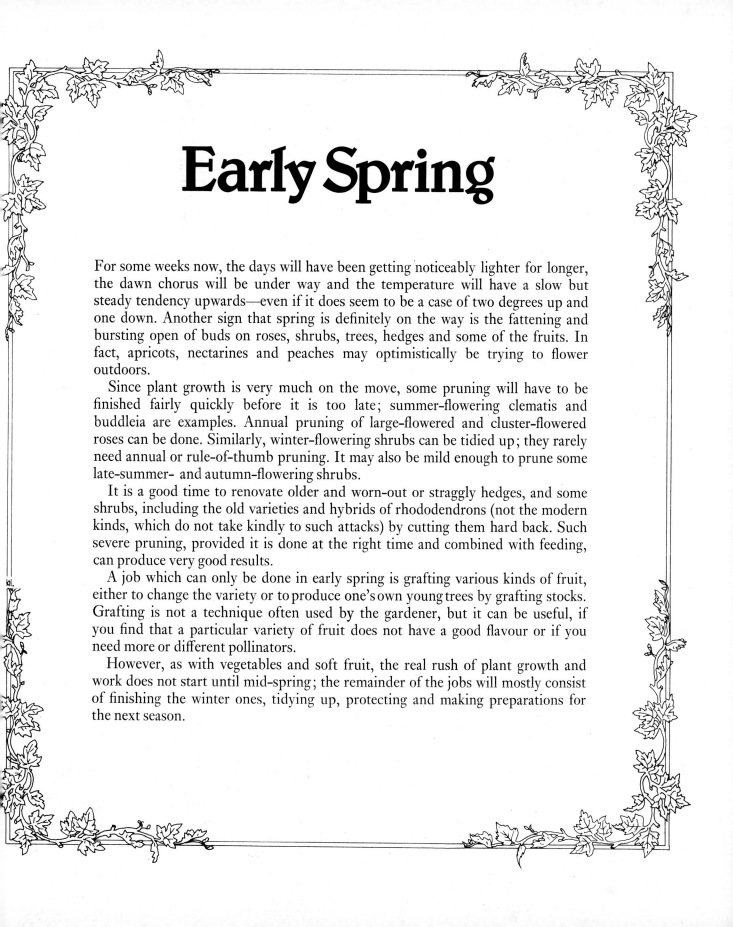

Early Spring

For some weeks now, the days will have been getting noticeably lighter for longer, the dawn chorus will be under way and the temperature will have a slow but steady tendency upwards—even if it does seem to be a case of two degrees up and one down. Another sign that spring is definitely on the way is the fattening and bursting open of buds on roses, shrubs, trees, hedges and some of the fruits. In fact, apricots, nectarines and peaches may optimistically be trying to flower outdoors.

Since plant growth is very much on the move, some pruning will have to be finished fairly quickly before it is too late; summer-flowering clematis and buddleia are examples. Annual pruning of large-flowered and cluster-flowered roses can be done. Similarly, winter-flowering shrubs can be tidied up; they rarely need annual or rule-of-thumb pruning. It may also be mild enough to prune some late-summer- and autumn-flowering shrubs.

It is a good time to renovate older and worn-out or straggly hedges, and some shrubs, including the old varieties and hybrids of rhododendrons (not the modern kinds, which do not take kindly to such attacks) by cutting them hard back. Such severe pruning, provided it is done at the right time and combined with feeding, can produce very good results.

A job which can only be done in early spring is grafting various kinds of fruit, either to change the variety or to produce one's own young trees by grafting stocks. Grafting is not a technique often used by the gardener, but it can be useful, if you find that a particular variety of fruit does not have a good flavour or if you need more or different pollinators.

However, as with vegetables and soft fruit, the real rush of plant growth and work does not start until mid-spring; the remainder of the jobs will mostly consist of finishing the winter ones, tidying up, protecting and making preparations for the next season.

At~a~glance diary

Prepare the soil for: planting outdoors

Plant: finish planting deciduous trees, shrubs, climbers and roses; plant evergreens and the hardier grey-leaved shrubs

Prune: large-flowered, cluster-flowered and climbing roses; winter-flowering cherry (Prunus subhirtella autumnalis), Garrya elliptica, heather (Erica carnea in variety), laurustinus (Viburnum tinus), Mahonia Charity, sarcococca, Viburnum Dawn and V. farreri, winter sweet (Chimonanthus praecox), witchhazel (Hamamelis mollis); late-summer-flowering shrubs: abelia (deciduous), Buddleia davidii, campsis, caryopteris, Ceratostigma willmottianum, fuchsia, heather (Calluna vulgaris in variety), hippophae, hydrangea, hypericum, indigofera, leycesteria, lupin (tree), potentilla, Sambucus nigra Aurea, solanum, sorbaria, southernwood (Artemisia abrotanum), spiraea, symphoricarpos, tamarisk; finish pruning fruit and summer-flowering clematis

Cut back hard: overgrown hedges; informal flowering hedges; old or overgrown shrubs grown as specimens; dogwood (cornus) and willow (salix)

Feed: all roses, summer-flowering shrubs and summer-flowering clematis; sites prepared for planting

Pollinate: apricots, peaches and nectarines

Protect: fruit trees and spring-flowering shrubs against pecking by birds; wall-grown apricots, peaches and nectarines against cold; newly planted shrubs and trees against rabbits, voles and hares

Pests and diseases: scab on apples and pears; greenfly in general; mildew on roses, gall on azaleas, wilt on young clematis

Routine work: inspect all for winter weather damage; firm in new plantings where lifted by frost; tie in grape vines

Increase: fruit by grafting. Clematis by layering

Jobs to do

Preparing the soil for planting

It is still not too late to plant the various kinds of shrubs and trees which would have been better put in during late autumn or early winter. If you are expecting an order to arrive from a nursery, have bought container-grown plants from a garden centre or have some plants heeled-in waiting for better weather, the soil can be prepared for these any time up to within a day or two of planting (see Mid-Autumn for details of method). Heavy soils may still be too wet for digging comfortably and any soil may be frozen, so always wait until it is possible to get a fork or a spade into it. If you find the soil difficult to penetrate, the plant roots will not find it easy either.

Planting

Once the dormant buds on woody plants begin to pop open and sprout stems and leaves, it is really too late for totally successful planting. As this will start happening shortly, you should plant roses, the hardy deciduous shrubs, including hedges and climbers, trees, vines and other fruit, as soon as possible. Towards the end of early spring is the time to plant many evergreens and a few of the hardiest grey-leaved shrubs, such as santolina and *Senecio greyi*. However, if there is some risk of a dry spring with strong cold winds, it would be better to wait until mid-spring or even early autumn, before planting these evergreens and evergreys (for details of planting all these see Late Autumn).

Pruning

The groups of plants which need pruning at this season are the large-flowered and cluster-flowered (hybrid tea and floribunda) and climbing roses, the late-summer-flowering shrubs and winter-flowering shrubs and trees. If the fruit and summer-flowering clematis have not been finished (or even started), their pruning should be completed as soon in early spring as possible, particularly as clematis may already have new shoots up to 30cm (12in) long (see Early and Late Winter for pruning details).

Senecio greyi is an extremely attractive shrub with evergreen leaves and bright yellow daisies in summer.

Roses Early spring is generally accepted as the time to prune the most popular group of roses: the large-flowered and cluster-flowered modern bush types. Some gardeners start doing it in mid- or late winter because they maintain that flowering starts earlier as a result. However, as the tips of the shoots, pruned or unpruned, are likely to be damaged or killed by cold, later pruning, when one can see any damage, may mean less damage and only one lot of pruning.

Rose buds generally start to sprout towards the end of early spring, so pruning should be started at the beginning of the season. Large-flowered kinds need moderately hard cutting back to stimulate as many and as strong new shoots as possible. Weak, spindly shoots should be cut back flush with their parent stem; shoots growing into the centre or across the bush should also be removed, together with dead shoots.

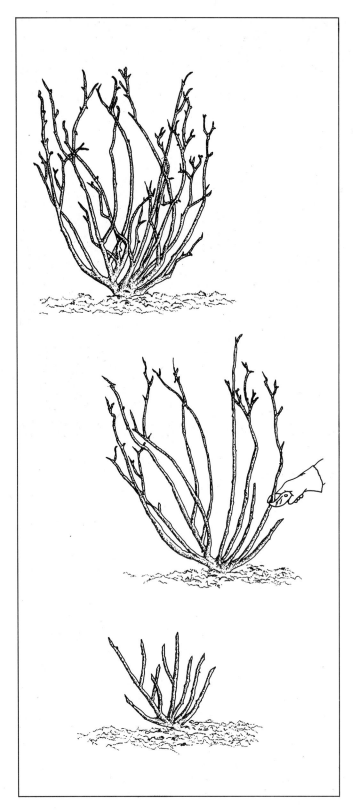

The remaining healthy and vigorous shoots should then be pruned to remove about half to two-thirds their length; try to place each cut so that the bud immediately below it points outwards and the one below that, too, if possible. It is often the case that the dormant bud you assumed would sprout and grow outwards to form a perfect, goblet-shaped bush either dies, gets attacked, knocked off or otherwise assaulted and the one below it grows beautifully, straight into the centre.

The majority of large-flowered roses produce a good display and plenty of blooms for the house if pruned like this, but the tall-growing, vigorous kinds such as Queen Elizabeth and Peace need lighter cutting, otherwise they get taller at the expense of flowers. For best results only one-third of the main stem is cut off and lesser stems are merely tipped. Occasionally, one of the old main stems can be cut down to ground level to encourage new wood.

Cluster-flowered rose pruning is not so simple; with some varieties the recommendation to remove last year's flowered stems can mean that virtually no growth is left above ground level. In order to produce the best show possible, pruning should ensure that the main stems are cut back to markedly differing lengths. For instance, those stems which are 'middle-aged' can be cut back moderately, to half to two-thirds their length, as the large-flowered kinds are. Any of last year's shoots produced at or close to ground level should have only about one-third of their length removed and the oldest stems, perhaps one, two or three of them, should be pruned hard to leave 7.5 or 10cm (3 or 4in) only. Besides this, there is the routine pruning to remove weak, diseased, crowded or crossing shoots, if any remain.

By treating each main stem individually like this, and pruning to different lengths, it is possible to maintain a renewal of growth each year throughout the bush so that strong new shoots are constantly being encouraged, while older ones which are still capable of flowering are retained to ensure as good a display as possible. For the details of pruning climbing roses, see Late Winter.

The winter-flowering shrubs and trees include autumn-flowering cherry (*Prunus subhirtella autumnalis*), *Garrya elliptica*, heather (*Erica carnea* in variety), laurustinus (*Viburnum tinus*), *Mahonia* Charity, sarcococca, *Viburnum* Dawn and *V. farreri*, winter sweet (*Chimonanthus praecox*) and witch hazel (*Hamamelis mollis*). All of these except the ericas need only a little pruning. Quite often you need not

Pruning roses: Large-flowered (hybrid tea) roses need to be pruned hard in early spring. Cuts should be made close to outward-pointing buds.

The winter-flowering heathers are some of the best small shrubs for providing colour at a dull time of the year. Erica carnea alba *will grow in chalky soil.*

do any pruning at all if they are growing naturally into an attractive shape, and they will still flower perfectly well.

However, most shrubs have some dead shoots, broken branches, thin, spindly shoots shorter than the rest, or crowded together and crossing over. Cutting away this sort of growth, even if you do nothing else, will always ensure that the shrub grows more healthily and has better flowers and leaves. At the same time you can deal with the odd long stem which protrudes far beyond the main body of the bush; if it is as strong as that it will not flower well in any case, so it is better removed altogether, back to its point of origin. You can also cut back some of the oldest shoots, once the shrubs have been planted a few years, to just above a new or strong younger shoot.

A general rule when pruning flowering shrubs is to cut off the shoots which have had flowers on them, with the object of inducing the shrub to produce new shoots to take their place and flower the coming season. However, winter-flowering shrubs on the whole are rather slow-growing and such cutting-back is more likely to mutilate their appearance and discourage growth, rather than encourage it. So, on the whole, the rule is not to cut off old flowering growth unless it comes into any of the categories that have just been mentioned above.

Viburnum farreri and *V.* Dawn tend to be awkwardly shaped and often do need to have their figures improved; laurustinus turns itself into a nicely rounded bush without help. The autumn-flowering cherry may stick a stem straight up out of the otherwise weeping head; don't hesitate to cut it right away, or the tree's head will become more and more grossly unbalanced.

The mahonia will probably produce new shoots at or near ground level as the central stem extends; if the latter becomes too tall, it can be cut right down and the younger shoots allowed to grow into its place.

Erica carnea and its varieties are pruned quite differently; as soon as flowering is really finished, but before new growth starts, they may be not so much pruned as sheared. Trim them straight across with shears to cut off the dead flowers and shoots; this need only be done in alternate years.

Garrya elliptica can be pruned in this season (see Pruning, Late Winter, for details); the remaining winter-flowering plants need not be pruned, except in occasional years in a general way.

The late-summer-flowering shrubs are generally considered to include those which flower in mid-summer, late summer and through early autumn into mid-autumn and pruning can be done towards the end of early spring or the beginning of mid-spring.

These shrubs generally flower on shoots produced earlier in the same season, i.e., a new shoot which starts to grow in early or mid-spring will bear flowers some time during the later part of summer or in autumn of the same year. As it is a principle of growth that the removal of shoots from a plant results in the plant replacing them with new shoots, so pruning in spring will—or should—automatically ensure that it will have a new crop of blossom later on. Therefore, if you do not have time to prune this type of shrub in the early part of spring and decide to make up for lost time by doing it in early summer, you will remove most of the new growth and flowering display. Not only that: the plant will try to make good the loss by developing a new batch of shoots, but too late for them to ripen by the time winter comes, so that tips will be killed, the shoots die back and disease infect the dead growth. The result is a weakly growing, poorly flowering shrub which may never recover.

The late-summer-flowering shrubs to prune towards the end of early spring include the following:

Abelia deciduous Prune only to tidy, cut out weak and straggling growth and one or two of the oldest shoots; regular annual pruning not necessary.

Berberis deciduous Prune only those with coloured leaves, e.g., Rose Glow, Aurea, and purple-leaved kinds except the dwarf form, since the young leaves and stems have the best colouring. Cut the main stems to strong new side-shoots and occasionally cut out one or two of the oldest shoots completely.

Buddleia davidii and varieties (butterfly bush)   Cut last year's long shoots back hard to leave a length of stem with only three or four dormant buds on it. In cold districts wait until mid-spring.

Campsis This is mostly spur-pruned: the new shoots are cut back to stumps with two buds on them, once the main shoots have filled the space available, but a few new shoots are left at their full length in suitable positions to clothe the support and the plant.

Caryopteris Cut flowered shoots moderately hard to leave about 23cm (9in) of stem, and cut weak shoots back hard, to

Buddleia davidii, *the butterfly bush, blooms late in summer; other colours are deep purple, plum and white.*

leave a stub with one or two buds. In cold districts wait until mid-spring before you do this pruning.

Ceratostigma willmottianum (plumbago) Cut back hard almost to ground level; in cold seasons or districts leave until mid-spring.

Fuchsia In mild districts cut off dead shoots and parts of shoots now and cut live side-shoots back to one or two pairs of buds. In other districts and cold seasons leave this until mid-spring.

Heather (*Calluna vulgaris* in variety) Trim with shears to cut off the flowered shoots.

Hydrangea (round headed) in variety Cut off old flower-heads to just above a pair of good buds; cut back some of the oldest shoots to ground level and those shoots killed by cold. Thin new shoots coming from ground level, otherwise they will be crowded.

Hippophae Hardly any pruning; remove weak shoots.

Hypericum Cut back the tall kinds hard so that last season's new shoots are reduced to a quarter of the length. Be careful with *H*. x *moseranum*; remove dead shoots only when new ones start to sprout.

Indigofera Annual pruning is not essential but better flowering will be obtained by cutting last season's new side-shoots back to leave stubs to produce new stems. Dead tips should be cut off and weak shoots removed to avoid overcrowding.

Leycesteria Remove some of the oldest stems at ground level and cut back last season's flowered growth by about half. In cold districts and seasons wait until mid-spring.

Lupin, tree Cut out the oldest stems and weak shoots completely and cut the strongest growth from last season by a half to two-thirds.

Potentilla, tall kinds to 1.5m (5ft) Cut to ground level to produce small, bushy and very floriferous plants or prune in mid-autumn.

Sambucus nigra Aurea (yellow-leaved elder) Cut last season's new shoots back to leave stubs 5 or 7.5cm (2 or 3in) long, so that plenty of new foliage is produced.

Solanum Every year, before new growth begins to appear, the weakest shoots should be cut back hard to leave one or two buds, and some of last year's strongest shoots pruned to leave three or four buds. Choice of shoot for cutting should ensure that the space allowed for growth is covered adequately and evenly.

Sorbaria Prune very hard, almost to ground level, leaving stubs with strong buds on them

Southernwood (*Artemisia abrotanum*) Prune last year's new growth to leave only 1.2cm (½in) stubs of it. Do not cut into growth older than this.

Spiraea, late-sumer-flowering kinds Cut last season's shoots back very hard to within a few centimetres (inches) of ground level; in some years cut out completely one or two of the oldest shoots also.

Symphoricarpos (snowberry) Cut out the weakest, oldest and straggling shoots completely and thin the remainder, making all cuts to ground level.

Tamarisk, autumn-flowering Cut last season's new growth back to leave stubs with dormant buds on them.

This list does not include all the summer-flowering shrubs shown in the table below, because some are more safely pruned in mid-spring.

Cutting back hard

Old deciduous hedges which have got rather gaunt and bare at the base can still be cut back hard in early spring, down to half or even less, of their height. Sometimes better results are obtained doing it just before new growth starts, rather than at the beginning of the dormancy period. Furthermore, you can remove growth killed by the winter's cold at the same time. Dormant buds, low down, will sprout as a result of the hard cutting.

If evergreen hedges are to be treated, early or, preferably, mid-spring is the time to cut them, but very hard cutting back is generally not advisable. The cypresses and brooms in particular object to this treatment and may die as a result. It is quite enough to remove about half the height of a hardy evergreen hedge and only about one-third of the sensitive ones. If the hedge has got too broad, as well as too high, wait until the second spring before cutting the sides, so that the vertical growth has a chance to grow and keep the hedge going while the sides recover from drastic trimming.

Informal flowering hedges which bloom from mid-summer onwards should be cut back now before growth really gets going. Cut last year's flowered shoots off to leave stubs a few centimetres (inches) long, on which there are dormant buds. Slow-growing hedges of this kind need not be trimmed except to cut back long straggling shoots now.

Individual shrub specimens which have grown tall or rather old can be rejuvenated by hard cutting at this time; *Buddleia davidii* and varieties and the tall hypericums can be pruned to leave stubs at ground level late in early spring. Doing this every few years is an alternative to moderate pruning every year. Hippophae, too, can be cut down to about 90cm (36in). The older and hardier rhododendron hybrids and varieties will tolerate cutting back to about 60-90cm (24-36in).

There is another reason for hard cutting back in spring, if the shrubs concerned have attractively coloured bark. There are varieties of dogwood (cornus) and willow (salix) which have brilliantly red, orange or yellow bark on the young shoots. If such plants are cut down hard to leave about 15cm (6in) of stem, they will produce a great number of these young shoots; all or about half of last year's shoots can be pruned, depending on how ruthless you feel.

Feeding

Roses can be given their first feed of the growing season as soon as pruning is finished. You can use one of the proprietary compound fertilizers, or a general one which is high in potash, to help with flowering. Summer-flowering shrubs and the later summer-flowering clematis can also be fed with similar fertilizers. If you still have shrubs or trees to put in, dress the site with bonemeal about a week before planting, forking it in evenly at about 120g per sq m (4oz per sq yd). Give hedges and shrubs which have been hard-pruned a dressing of a general compound fertilizer, forking or hoeing it in if practicable, or watering it in.

Pollinating
The only blossom likely to be out at this time of the year is that of peaches, nectarines and apricots. Such fruits are natives of much warmer climates than the temperate zone and so flower earlier, with the certainty of being pollinated

Peaches are self-fertile, but they flower so early in the year that hand-pollination is advisable in many cases.

by insects which also come out of their winter hibernation much earlier. Pollinators from temperate climates do not appear in large quantities until mid-spring, so you must help the process of fertilization with a child's paint-brush, doing it preferably in the middle of a sunny day.

Protecting
The fruit and the shrubs which have had cover on them all winter to guard against bullfinches, sparrows and other birds nipping out the flower or fruit buds should be gone over carefully, as the birds can do a lot of damage now, at the end of winter. The forsythia and flowering cherry displays can be non-existent as a result of bud pecking, and sprays and protective webbing may need renewing.

Apricots, peaches and nectarines growing with wall protection may already be in flower, or just coming up to it, and if you want to be certain of a crop, you should insulate against frost and cold winds. A polythene net dropped in front of them from battens on the wall will do the job, or you can have a more elaborate arrangement with clear plastic sheeting. Remove it as soon as the temperature goes up, otherwise any pollinating insects about cannot do their work.

Treating pests and diseases
In early spring there is little more to do to woody plants than examine them to discover how they are. New growth will only just be starting to appear, so pests and diseases will not yet be visible in large quantities. Greenfly, of course, may start to hatch from their over-wintering eggs, in town gardens and others where the district is mild or the season an early one. The opening buds of roses, apples and pears are likely to be their main targets.

The fungus disease, scab, on apples and pears (a different strain on the latter) may start to infect leaves as they unfold, if temperature and humidity are high enough, but mid-spring is usually the season when it becomes really dangerous. Mildew may attack the new growth of roses, especially if it were present the previous year. Fruit can be infected by mildew and there are different mildews according to which fruit is being infected. However, they can all be treated with the same chemicals. If mildew does appear, it is worth removing the ailing growth now, cutting off the shoot well below the infection, even if it does mean removing apparently healthy growth.

The fungus disease on azaleas which makes the leaves become thick and curled up, with grey bloom on the surface, is called azalea gall; cutting off the affected parts is usually all that need be done. Gall does not appear on outdoor azaleas very much; the indoor potted types are more likely to get gall as it thrives in close, humid conditions (see Controls and Treatments section for details of chemical sprays, and the spray chart in Mid-Winter).

General work
If it has not been done before, taking a good look round the plants is advisable, to discover broken branches, stakes which have been blown askew, loosened ties, trees which have been wind-rocked (so that a hollow full of water has formed round the base of the trunk), and freshly planted trees and shrubs which have been lifted out of the soil as a result of the action of frost. Any of these troubles left unrepaired will at best result in a damaged and weakened

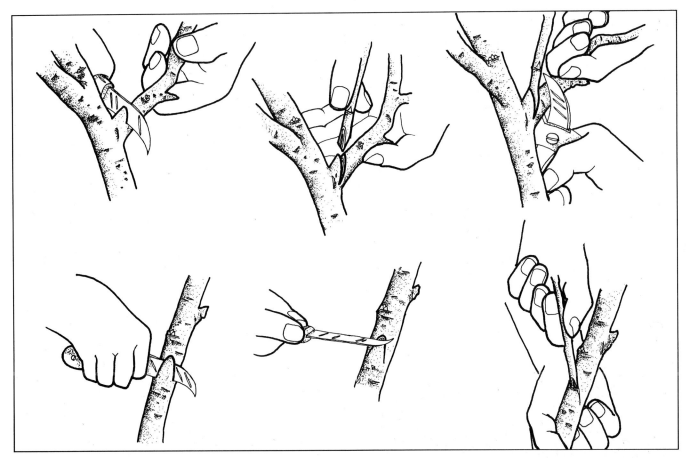

plant and at worst a dead one. Wind-rocking causes some of the most serious trouble, because the collected water starts a rot of the bark of the trunk. Once the bark has been killed all the way round, it is only a matter of time before the tree dies.

Check that protective coverings and barriers against cold are still intact and in place; although this is the beginning of the spring some of the coldest weather of the winter can occur during the next four or five weeks.

The main stems of grape vines, which were loosened and allowed partially to hang down in mid winter can now be tied back in position again.

Increasing

Early spring is the recommended season for grafting fruit trees. The grafting the gardener will most likely want to do will be the kind that changes the variety of a mature tree and this is most frequently done with apples and pears. By now the sap has begun to run again and the chance of the grafts 'taking' is much more certain than at any other season.

Framework grafting: If a fruit tree is to be changed to another variety, its branches are cut back and grafted by two methods. Above: Stub-grafting. The scion is cut into a wedge shape and the branch forced open, then cut off just above the graft. Below: Side-cleft. A tongue is lifted and the scion's end is tapered.

For grafting you will need a really sharp, straight-bladed, grafting knife (not an ordinary penknife and not one with a curved blade), grafting wax (proprietary hot and cold waxes can be bought from garden shops) and a brush; a rag always seems to be useful, too.

On a mature tree with a cup-shaped arrangement of main branches, the latter should be left to almost their complete length, so that the growth at the end of each is not less than two years old. The side-shoots and side branches should be cut back to about 20cm (8in) long.

The pattern of grafting should be herring-bone, so that the new branches come out alternately on each side of a main branch; any original side branches which do not fit into this pattern should be removed completely. So, too, should any main branches growing into the centre of the tree or straight upwards; if any are too close, now is the time to remove one here and there.

The secret of successful grafting is to get what are known as the cambium layers matching. The cambium is a layer of tissue composed of cells which divide and create new woody cells, just below the bark; in most plants the cambium is bright green, The sloping cuts made in both scion and stock expose as much of this layer as possible and so increase the chances of the graft being successful.

The scion is the new variety to be grafted on to the parent tree, or stock, and for the average bush apple or pear on dwarfing stock, about a hundred scions will be required. You should have already obtained them (see Early Winter) and they can now be cut so that they are about 10 buds long. For a stub graft, the end of the scion should be cut to form a short wedge. The side branch or side-shoot to be

Mahonis japonica *is strongly fragrant, like lily-of-the-valley. It flowers on and off all through winter and early spring, and sometimes in late autumn, too.*

grafted has a sloping cut made partially through its upper side; this cut is pulled open and the scion pushed into it, matching the cut surfaces. Once the scion is in, the stub can be cut back to just above the graft and grafting wax painted completely over the whole stub and cut so that there are no gaps at all.

If there is no stub in a suitable position, a side-cleft grafting may be used instead. Cut the branch to be grafted to lift a tongue of bark and wood, cut the tip of the tongue off and push the scion in with the cut surfaces facing and matching. The end of the scion for this type of graft should have a single flat, tapered surface; finish by waxing, as before. The ends of the main branches should be stub grafted.

After grafting, as the tree begins to grow, sucker shoots will appear from trunk and main branches; these suckers should be removed while still only a few centimetres (inches) long.

Clematis can still be layered, but mid-spring will be too late (see Late Autumn for method), so do it early in the season.

Plants in flower

Apricot, Camellia, Flowering cherry, Clematis armandii, Corylopsis, Flowering currant, Forsythia, Gorse, Japonica, Jasmine (winter-flowering, Jasminum nudiflorum), Laurustinus, Magnolia stellata, Mahonia japonica, Pieris, Peach, Rhododendrons in variety, Skimmia, Spiraea thunbergii

Fruits in store

Apple, Pear, Quince

Mid-Spring

Spring might have been a little hesitant in appearing during the last few weeks, but there will be no doubt about its presence by now. Cherries, pears and plums will be in flower, wall-grown peaches and nectarines will be setting their fruit, many shrubs and trees will be blossoming. New leaves and shoots will be sprouting everywhere, and so will the weeds. The places most likely to need urgent weeding will be rose-beds, hedge bottoms, trained fruit grown against walls or as dividers and specimen trees grown in beds.

Pruning will continue to be a major activity. There will be some planting and this is also the time to start layering various shrubs. Seeds which have been stratified through the winter, and others, can be sown; there may be cuttings to take in sheltered gardens.

Although woody plants are apparently not much affected by bad weather, it is only short spells of bad weather to which they are immune. Prolonged cold, drought, waterlogging and wind take an equally prolonged and severe toll, but it does not show on this type of plant until months, perhaps even a year, have passed. Unfortunately, by that time, some other type of unfavourable weather may have ensued and the compound damage results in a small, unhappy plant, if it lives at all.

It is extremely important to foresee these problems and take steps to ameliorate them before they have lasted more than a week or two. For instance, in early spring, strong, cold wind, bright sun and drought can set in and continue for six weeks or more. The effect of this on newly-planted evergreens can be death, unless you put up a barrier in the path of the prevailing wind, keep the soil moist and spray the top growth every day.

Friends and foes in the insect world will be on the move, like everything else; disease spores will be floating about in their millions, and there may still be trouble from birds and animals. A variety of jobs will be started now, to be carried on through the season; these include blueing hydrangeas, making compost, mowing orchard swards and deadheading flowering shrubs.

At~a-glance diary

Prepare the soil for: planting outdoors

Plant: the hardier grey-leaved shrubs and evergreens; finish any planting left from early spring; young shrubs, roses and trees grown from seed

Prune: large/cluster-flowered and climbing roses if in cold districts or if the season is late; finish planting winter-flowering shrubs and late-summer-flowering kinds. Also prune: Buddleia globosa, evergreen berberis, brooms, camellia ceanothus, flowering currant, daisy bush (olearia haastii) dogwood, forsythia, fuchsia heather (calluna and Erica carnea), hebe (shrubby veronica), hibiscus, hydrangea, ivy, lavender, lavender cotton (santolina), tree mallow (lavatera), mahonia, pyracantha (firethorn), romneya (Californian poppy), rue, Senecio greyi, yucca

Disbud: peach, nectarine, vine

Cut back hard: evergreen hedges

Deadhead: rhododendrons and pieris

Pot: rooted vine-eyes

Feed: planting sites; roses, summer-flowering shrubs and summer-flowering clematis if not done in early spring; hedges and shrubs cut back hard for rejuvenation

Blue: hydrangea

Water: newly planted specimens, plants growing close to walls or fences

Support: climbers

Protect: new shoots against frost, remove protective mulches from tender plants

Thin: apricot, peach, nectarine grown against walls

Increase: tree fruit by grafting; shrubs, climbers and roses by layering; a variety of plants by seed

Weed: where necessary

Mow: orchard swards

Compost heap: start to build

Ring: pear trees

Pests and diseases: aphids (greenfly, blackfly, mealy-aphid, etc) caterpillars, vine weevil, mildew, scab, rose black spot, peach leaf curl, clematis wilt; remove grease-bands from fruit trees

Jobs to do

Preparing the soil for planting

Mid-spring is a better time to plant some of the shrubs mentioned in early spring, and there are others which should not be planted until now, so soil will need to be prepared for these in the usual way by forking it, clearing it of winter weeds and mixing in fertilizer (see Feeding).

Planting

Finish any planting left from early spring. You should be able to plant the hardier grey-leaved shrubs towards the end of mid-spring and most of the evergreens at any time (see tables for tender species). However, if you are in the middle of a cold, sunny period, and you have somewhere to heel in open-ground plants, it is better to wait until the weather improves. Warm, showery springs are ideal for planting, but drought combined with cold wind can be as damaging as when it is combined with heat, in summer.

Shrubs, roses and trees grown from seed sown last spring can now be planted in their permanent positions (see Planting, Late Spring).

If planting in bad conditions is unavoidable, do all that you can to insulate the plants from them. Mix coarse sand and granulated peat into wet soil to mop up and drain at the same time. Remember that evergreens lose water through their leaves constantly and while their roots are settling down, they will not be absorbing water to replace that being lost by the top growth. The result is brown leaves or brown needles, particularly on the windward side. A daily spray overhead with water is essential in cold or windy dry weather, together with a wind barrier and some soil watering.

Pruning

If you were unable to finish pruning the roses in early spring, you should do so in the first week of this season. In all but cold districts, shoots and leaves will be developing fast; pruning once the plant is growing again weakens it. Those with chilly gardens will not normally expect to prune roses until now in any case, but wherever your garden

The brooms are handsome shrubs which cover themselves in flower in late spring and summer. Cytisus scoparius Andreanus grows to about 2.4m (7ft).

is, be guided by the stage of growth the bushes have reached. Pruning just as the buds begin to swell is a good time, although, if you have a lot of roses, you may have to start earlier, in order to get round them all before it is too late.

Any of the winter-flowering shrubs which were not pruned in early spring should be dealt with early this season, also the late-summer-flowering kinds as listed (see **Pruning, Early Spring**). In addition the following can now be pruned; they include some of the more tender species and some evergreens, as well as the early-spring-flowering shrubs and less hardy, late-summer-flowering subjects.

If in doubt about pruning any shrub, mid-spring is usually safe; although many do not need annual pruning, they do occasionally, every five years or so, need cutting to a better shape, restricting to the space provided instead of overflowing it and dead, ailing, crowded or stunted shoots cleared out.

Buddleia globosa This tends to become rather leggy and awkwardly shaped, so it should be cut back by about half towards the end of mid-spring, every few years, instead of pruning later, after flowering. However, in cold districts this may kill it, and it would be better to start again from rooted cuttings.

Berberis, evergreen Cut some of the oldest shoots down to the ground so that the remainder have more air and light; also cut some other shoots down to the origin of strong one-year-old growth, but wait until flowering has finished before pruning. Do all this occasionally.

Broom (*Cytisus battandieri*) Regular pruning is not necessary, but occasional cutting back of straggling shoots and branches in mid-spring will improve its appearance.

Camellia (*japonica* types) If space has been outgrown by rather elderly specimens, cut back by about half or a little more; any other pruning is not necessary. These shrubs are amongst the best for arranging themselves in a shapely way and producing a mass of flowers. They are hardy enough to withstand several degrees of frost at least and can be covered in icicles without harm to the leaves or shoots.

Ceanothus, autumn-flowering Prune those with a wall backing them in mid-spring—if the weather is not cold—by cutting back strong-flowered shoots to leave about 30cm (12in) of stem. They also tend to grow a lot of short, weak, crossing shoots which do not flower and clutter up the bush, so these should be removed as well.

Currant, flowering (ribes) No regular pruning; prune to shape every few years and cut out old shoots to just above strong young shoots.

Daisy bush (*Olearia haastii*) Can be trimmed with the shears in mid-spring or cut back hard if you want the bush to put out a lot of new growth.

Dogwood (Cornus), see Pruning, Early Spring.

Forsythia Specimen bushes should have some of the flowered shoots cut back after flowering, to newly growing stems. If the bush is rather thick and overgrown in spite of this, the oldest shoots can be cut right down to the ground and others cut hard to let in light and air. Wall-grown forsythias, such as *F. suspensa*, need regular pruning every spring; the flowered shoots are cut back to a stub 5 or 7.5cm (2 or 3in) long.

Fuchsia By now most fuchsias will be showing some signs of life and dead shoots and dead shoot tips will be obvious; these should be removed and remaining side-shoots cut back to one or two pairs of dormant buds. Weak shoots should be cut right off.

Heather (calluna and *Erica carnea* in variety) If not already done in early spring, trim off the flowered shoots with shears, annually for calluna, alternate years for the ericas.

Hebe (shrubby veronica) Being evergreen, hebes must be treated with care. Prune every three years or so, late in mid-spring or in late spring, if they are outgrowing their space or getting leggy.

Hibiscus Pruning is usually not needed, but if they are getting too large, they can be pruned hard, by half their growth, early in mid-spring.

Hydrangea (round-headed) If pruning were not done at the end of early spring, it can be done early in this season by cutting off the old-flower-heads to just above a pair of good buds, removing some of the oldest shoots completely, and thinning out the new shoots, again to ground level. Alternatively, pruning can be done every few years, cutting the whole bush back to stubs with one or two buds on them.

Ivy Rarely needs any treatment, but if it is colonizing too much, trimming can be done now.

Lavender Cut back last season's shoots to within a couple of centimetres (about an inch) of their origin. Lavender tends to become leggy within a few years and should be replaced, but as it roots easily from cuttings this is no problem.

Lavender cotton (santolina) This can be cut back hard once a year, in spring, to just above the new growth which will be appearing by now. Alternatively, it can be trimmed two or three times in the growing season to keep it tidy.

Mahonia Mahonia japonica need not be pruned at all unless one of the main stems is getting rather leggy, in which case it can be cut low down and new shoots will come from the

The ceanothus are shrubs which deserve to be grown much more as they are one of the few with blue flowers.

base to fill the gap. Normally, however, it grows into a leafy, rounded shrub. *M. aquifolium* does not need pruning; *Mahonia* Charity can have one of its main stems cut down to near ground level if getting too tall as it produces shoots from the base without any fuss.

Tree mallow (*Lavatera arborea*) A fast-growing shrub, so cut back low down on each main shoot to where new growth is beginning to appear.

Pyracantha (firethorn) If it is wall-trained and has got rather large and untidy, it can be cut back hard into shape, though there will not be any flowers for the coming season.

Romneya (Californian poppy) Being on the tender side, this may well have had all its stems killed during winter, but if not, they should be cut down practically to ground level. It will grow well again and can be regarded somewhat in the same way as herbaceous peonies.

Rue (*Ruta graveolens*) Last year's growth can be cut back hard, close to its base, so that it produces as much of its grey-blue ferny foliage as possible.

Senecio greyi Cut back towards the end of mid-spring, removing last year's growth to leave stubs. It is not essential to do all this every year; you can get away with simply cutting off straggling stems, those that are outgrowing the space and those lying on the ground. The latter will provide new plants as they will probably have rooted.

Willow (salix) see Pruning, Early Spring.

Yucca Remove all dead leaves every year at this time.

Disbudding

It could be said that disbudding is a form of pruning, as it involves the removal of shoots, but they are taken away when only 2.5 or 5cm (1 or 2in) long. Fan-trained peaches and vines grown against walls are treated like this during spring and later as needed. For peaches and nectarines, each side-shoot should have left on it, one new shoot at its base, one about half way along it to act as a 'feeder' (or replacement if need be), and the new growth at its tip, the leader. All the rest should be rubbed off, except the shoot growing immediately next to a fruit, which is pinched back to one leaf. Do this disbudding gradually in about three stages, to avoid shock to the tree. This treatment ensures the growth of new shoots for next year's crop and the prevention of bare leggy shoots which do not fruit.

Vines are disbudded in spring so that there is only one shoot left at each spur and one shoot at the end of the main branch, or rod. Wherever there is a pair of shoots, the weaker of the two is rubbed off. The remaining shoots on both peaches and vines are tied in as they grow, spacing them evenly.

Cutting back hard

Evergreen hedges that have become too tall and bare at the base can be rejuvenated now by removing about half their height (see Early Spring). Laurel hedges can be more drastically treated, if your district has warm, wet weather now, by cutting down to stumps about 30 or 45cm (12 or 18in) tall. You will have to do without the hedge for a season or so, but it is a strong shrub and will quickly produce new growth, which you can keep bushy at the base from the start.

Deadheading

You may have already cut some flowers in the natural course of events for the home, but any that have finished on the rhododendrons and pieris should be cut off, otherwise the plants' energy is concentrated on forming seed instead of new flowering shoots.

Opposite: *Peaches are thinned from the time when they are marble-sized, to one every 23cm (9in) square.* Below: *The firethorns (pyracantha spp.) set berries which often last through the winter.*

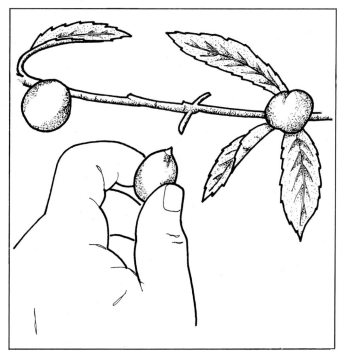

Potting

Vine-eyes, put to root in late winter, should now be ready for potting into a 13.5cm (5in) pot of good potting compost. They should be kept protected.

Feeding

Sites prepared for planting should have bonemeal mixed into them at 120g per sq m (4oz per sq yd), if possible a week or so in advance, otherwise the day before. Try to avoid mixing the fertilizer with the soil as you plant, because some roots will inevitably come into contact with the fertilizer; this results in 'burning' and the root dies back.

If it has not been done in early spring, feed roses, summer-flowering shrubs and summer-flowering clematis now; also give a general compound fertilizer to hedges and shrubs cut back hard for rejuvenation.

Blueing

At the beginning of mid-spring, if you want blue hydrangeas rather than pink or red, you can begin to water the soil round the plants with a solution of aluminium sulphate and iron sulphate. Mix 7g ($\frac{1}{4}$oz) of each in 4.5 litres (1 gal) soft water, leave the solution to stand for a few hours and then give each plant 9 litres (2 gal), watered all over the area which the roots are likely to have reached. Apply every week until flowering time and then give one more dose at some point in early autumn.

Watering

You should keep an eye on anything which is newly planted, particularly in dry cold springs, and especially evergreens, wisteria, hydrangea, and any plant planted close to a wall or fence. They are all very vulnerable to a few days without water, unless planted in rather wet soil, and a gentle shower from the hose for a couple of hours every few days until there is rain will help them survive without any harm through a dry period.

Supporting

If you have not already got supports in place for some of the climbers, you should get them fixed early this season. Clematis will be growing very fast and may be halfway up a wall; in warm gardens eccremocarpus shoots may be long enough to start flowering. Panels of plastic-covered trellis, or horizontal wires spaced 30cm (12in) apart, attached to wall nails, are amongst the strongest and most convenient supports for wall climbers.

If you have climbing roses, wisteria, Russian vine (*Polygonum baldschuanicum*) or honeysuckle scrambling over pergolas, archways or fences, make sure that they are stout enough to support what will eventually be a considerable weight of vegetation when dry, and half as much again when wet. Summer gales can be almost as fierce as winter gales and, once these climbing plants are blown down, their effect will never be the same again for the rest of the season. Repairing the damage is such a thankless and complicated job that it is tempting to cut everything off at ground level and be without any display until next year. So, if you make everything much stronger than you think it need be, you will be greatly relieved later on.

Protecting

New growth on any plant is vulnerable to cold but, unfortunately, frost at night, and even during the day, is still possible. Young shoots caught by frost will die back from the tip and can then be infected by fungus diseases, such as grey mould; this compounds the damage, and flowering will be delayed. Although it is probably not practicable to protect all the new growth, you will have favourite shrubs, fruit or roses, and plastic netting, newspapers or thin material (cotton or nylon) can be draped over them until the risk has passed.

Protective mulches which have been put over the crowns of tender plants, such as fuchsias, eccremocarpus, romneya, solanum and ceratostigma, in late autumn, should be removed carefully, as the plants will have started to sprout at the beginning of this season.

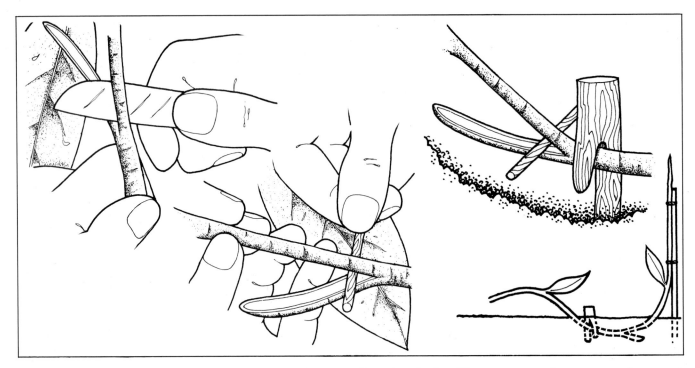

Thinning

Apricots, peaches and nectarines, which are wall-grown, will have set their blossom by now in all but the coldest gardens; when the fruits are about the size of a marble, you can start thinning. Do it gradually over about two weeks until they begin to 'stone', the sign of which is that the fruit stops swelling. After this, they will have a small natural drop and you can then do a final thinning, if necessary.

Start by taking off fruit growing towards the wall, then take one away from every pair and eventually remove some of the remainder so that there are about 12 peaches to every sq m (sq yd) and 20 nectarines for the same area.

Apricots have a heavy natural drop and should not be thinned until after this, when they can be spaced in the same way as nectarines.

Increasing

There is still time to graft, as the bark will lift easily all the time the sap is rising, from early to late spring; if, however, the buds on the scion start to sprout, the scions will no longer take and the grafting cannot be done for another year.

Another method of increase, used on ornamentals, is layering, and there are many shrubs, climbers and roses which can be easily propagated in this way. Choose a good shoot which grew last year and which is growing close to the ground; make a cut upwards on the underside, opposite a joint, through part of the stem. Pull the stem down to the

Layering shrubs: Choose a young shoot near to the ground, make a cut partially through it on the underside, wedge open, and pin down into good soil or compost.

soil so that the cut is in contact with it and peg the shoot down or hold it in place with a stone. The cut should be made several centimetres (inches) from the tip. When the layer is pegged down, the end of the shoot should be bent gently upward and tied to a cane.

If you layer the plants now, they should have rooted and be ready for lifting and planting in the autumn. Many will root if layered any time between spring and autumn, but doing it now does mean that they can be planted at one of the most suitable times. Plants to layer include rambling and climbing roses, rhododendrons, viburnums, magnolia, laurel, spotted laurel and various other evergreens. It is worth trying this method on any shrub with conveniently low-growing shoots; even if you do not want the rooted layers as new plants, they increase the visual effect of the parent plant so that it provides an even better show.

Many woody plants can be grown from seed sown in spring, and mid-spring is probably the best period. It can be sown outdoors in a seed bed, where the soil has been dug in winter, and then raked to crumb-like consistency on the day of sowing. As seedlings have a particular need for the mineral nutrient phosphorus, superphosphate should be mixed in a week or so before, at 30g per sq m (1oz per sq yd). Seeds of the more tender species can be sown in cold frames using seed compost and seed pans or direct into the frame soil suitably prepared. Germination may take any time from a few days to a year.

Seeds of some plants need stratifying (see Mid Autumn). Top-fruit stones and pips will germinate well but the resultant plant will not be the same variety as its parent. Moreover, seedlings tend to be very vigorous and either do not come into bearing at all or do so after ten years or more. Seedlings of ornamentals will also be different from their parents, and if you want exactly similar varieties or hybrids, you will have to use vegetative methods of increase: layering, cuttings, budding or division.

Weeding

From now until the end of autumn, weeding will be necessary at intervals, but it is not nearly such a problem as in the kitchen garden or where the herbaceous plants are grown. If you like clean rose-beds, there is a weedkiller which will keep the weeds at bay for the season, or you can use mulches. Ground-cover plants are another possible way of keeping down weeds, but it does mean trampling on them when pruning and feeding the roses can be awkward.

The same weedkiller can be used round certain shrubs, climbers, hedges and fruit, as the makers direct, but a better method is to mulch heavily. It does the plants a power of good as well. Of course, if you have specimen shrubs, trees and fruit growing in a lawn, or if you have an orchard down to grass, the weed problem can be ignored, if you like. Lawn weeds can be left alone, provided they do not overwhelm the grass, and an orchard mixture of grasses and clovers will effectively keep out other plants (see Controls and Treatments section for chemical weedkillers).

Grass cutting

Orchards down to grass should be cut now and kept at about 10cm (4in) until the end of mid-summer, when they can be left, though for convenience at fruit-picking time; the grass is probably better kept short.

Making a compost heap

Do not put prunings on the compost heap unless summer ones, of soft green shoots; those with bark or hard, tough tissue should be burnt. The resulting ash will be rich in potassium.

You can make the heap out of the orchard mowings, weeds, dead flowers, leaves (not evergreens, they are too tough to rot down well) and soft prunings. Build it with 23cm (9in) layers of vegetative material alternating with

5cm (2in) soil layers, up to 120-150cm (48-60in) high, enclose it with wood or polythene and cover when finished. It should be ready for use in autumn.

Ringing

Pear trees can be ringed at blossom time; see Late Spring for details.

Treating pests and diseases

This is the season when greenfly and caterpillars will eat blossom as well. Vine weevils start eating holes in the edges

The barberries (berberis spp.) are splendid shrubs, with flowers, berries and good leaves, some evergreen.

of rhododendron leaves nearest the ground; slugs will attack the new shoots of fuchsias, hydrangeas, romneya and tree peonies. Rabbits may also attack these succulent shoots. Mildew may appear or continue to spread on roses, apples and pears, and infected shoots should be cut out. Scab on apples and pears may infect leaves and bad infections are likely to occur in warm, rainy springs. Rose black spot may appear or continue to spread. If peach-leaf curl on peaches, nectarines, almonds and apricots appears, pick off infected leaves and cut out infected growth as necessary; destroy all diseased prunings.

Young clematis may go off suddenly with clematis wilt; cut the shoots concerned down to ground level as soon as seen and cover the cut surfaces with a fungicidal wound-sealing compound. Spray new growth with a fungicide.

If you had grease-bands on the trunks of fruit trees, they can be removed now, as they will not be needed until late summer, when the adult winter moths begin to appear.

Chemical fungicides and insecticides for all these troubles are given in the Controls and Treatments section.

Skilfully placed and selected shrubs, mingled with trees, give a garden depth, as well as colour and line.

Plants in flower

Apple (early varieties and crab apples), Apricot, Berberis in variety, Cherry (ornamental and fruiting), Clematis alpina and C. armandii, Corylopsis, Flowering currant, Cytisus × kewensis and C.praecox, Damson, Eccremocarpus (shelter), Forsythia, Fothergilla, Gorse, Greengage, Heathers (tree), Japonica, Mahonia aquifolium, Magnolia in variety, Medlar, Osmanthus, Peach (bush) Pear, Pieris, Plum, Quince, Rhododendron in variety, Skimmia, Spiraea × arguta and S.thunbergii, Viburnum burkwoodii and V. carlesii

Fruits in store

Apple, Pear

Late Spring

Late spring is one of the best seasons for display as far as shrubs are concerned. Many of them burst into full flower now and rhododendrons and azaleas will be at their most beautiful. If your garden contains alkaline soil, you can still have a marvellous display and a greater variety of flower and leaf shape than gardeners who rely solely on rhododendrons. Much of the fruit will be in full bloom, too, and it would be hard to beat an apple orchard on a sunny day for beauty. Some of the smaller trees, such as laburnum, the Judas tree and hawthorn, come into flower to join the show. Wisteria, clematis and the early climbing or rambling roses are in bloom now as well.

However, there is another side to every story; tree fruit is the target for a great number of insects and fungus diseases. Roses are another main source of food for these pests, and the rest of the shrubs, trees and climbers have their own special predators. The main hatch or appearance of all these occurs in late spring, so that much finger-and-thumb work and spraying may have to be done for the next few weeks. If controlled early in the growing season, there should be no serious trouble for the rest of it.

There is still a good deal of surgery required, mainly on shrubs, but also on peaches, vines, some of the tree fruit and the fast-growing hedges. Pruning, pinching back, trimming, disbudding, deadheading and cutting away remaining winter-killed shoots should be done. None of this is absolutely obligatory; most of the plants will produce some flowers or fruit if left to themselves but the quantity and quality will gradually tail off over the years. The life of a plant will also be short if its growth is not judiciously controlled with the knife or secateurs.

At~a~glance diary

Prepare the soil for: planting

Plant: tender and some grey-leaved shrubs; container-grown shrubs; seedlings

Prune: (if necessary) berberis, Clematis alpina, C. armandii, C. montana, corylopsis, forsythia, fothergilla, tree heather, japonica, osmanthus, Senecio greyi, skimmia, Spiraea x arguta, tamarisk (Tamarix tetrandra), cistus (rock rose), fuchsia, phlomis (Jerusalem sage), apricot, grape vine

Pinch back: (continued above)

Disbud: Morello cherry, nectarine, peach, vine

Deadhead: azalea, camellia, lilac, pieris, rhododendron

Trim: hedges of gorse, hawthorn, Lonicera nitida, myrobalan (Prunus cerasifera), privet

Mulch: shrubs, climbers, roses, trees, wall-grown peaches and vines; tree fruit in dry soil

Water: wall-grown plants; newly planted specimens

Thin: apricot, nectarine, peach fruits; vine flower clusters

Support: wall-grown plants

Ring: apple

Pests and diseases: bacterial canker (cherry and plum), blackfly, black spot (rose), capsid, caterpillars, sawfly caterpillars (apple and pear), clematis wilt, fireblight, greenfly, grey mould, holly-leaf miner, leaf hopper, leaf sucker, mealy plum aphis, pear leaf-blister mite, pear midge, peony wilt, red spider mite, scab, slug

Routine work: weed, build compost heap, blue hydrangea, mow orchard sward

Jobs to do

Preparing the soil for planting

Late spring is the only safe time to plant some of the grey-leaved or tender shrubs, if ordered from a nursery; you may be buying container-grown plants in any case, so a little soil preparation will probably be necessary. Problems with frost and waterlogging should no longer occur and the difficulty in late spring, when forking the soil, may be hardness due to drought. However, this is easily remedied. Most weeds will be seedlings, also easily dealt with. Remember to add phosphatic fertilizer some days before planting (see Mid-Autumn for details of soil preparation).

Clematis are justifiably popular climbing plants, and jackmanii *is one of the best of its colour.*

Planting

Shrubs which should not be planted before late spring include cistus (rock rose), fuchsia, romneya (Californian poppy), ceratostigma (plumbago) and phlomis (Jerusalem sage). In cold districts, hebe and hibiscus are better left to the beginning of late spring before planting.

Seed which was sown in mid-spring may have produced seedlings large enough to handle by now. If so, they can be transplanted to a nursery bed where they should be left for about a year before moving to their permanent places.

From now until the end of summer, there is always the possibility of heat, combined with drought, and to endure survival of newly planted shrubs under these conditions you should have a look at them every few days and supply water if need be. Container-grown plants, whether fruits, shrubs, trees or climbers can, in theory, be planted at any time during late spring or summer, but they do seem to have a struggle to establish and need a good deal of cosseting.

Pruning

Mid-spring pruning should be finished as soon as possible; the main group of shrubs to be pruned during this season are those flowering from early spring to the middle of late spring, as named in the following list. You can do some pruning when cutting flowering sprays for the house; make sure that the cut is made just above a strong, new shoot.

Berberis, deciduous or evergreen Cut some of the oldest shoots down to ground level, cut flowered shoots back to strong new growth and thin out the remainder. This need only be done every three years or so.

Clematis The *montana* types can be cut back hard immediately after flowering to leave a few centimetres (inches) of the flowered growth every year or they can be pruned every four years or so in the same way, but further back, to the oldest growth. If *C. alpina* and its varieties needs treatment, do it after flowering, to thin out the oldest shoots and cut back others to strong new growth, also every few years. *C. armandii* can grow extremely large against a sunny wall but is a little tender, and does not take well to any more pruning than occasional thinning out and cutting back to the space available.

Corylopsis Virtually no pruning needed, as its habit of growth is naturally tidy and well-spaced but occasional removal of weak shoots and those which are old and hardly flowering improves its appearance even more.

Forsythia If late in flowering or not yet pruned, forsythia should be pruned now; remove flowering sprays and thin out remainder (see Mid-Spring for details).

Fothergilla A charming shrub, with its white chimney-sweep's brushes of flowers, it hardly needs any cutting beyond the removal of dead shoots, weak ones and any which cross or are too close to each other.

Tree heathers, spring-flowering (*Erica arborea, E. australis,* etc.) These can be left alone and will still flower well but are bushier and more floriferous if cut back after flowering by about 30-60cm (12-24in).

Japonica (chaenomeles) The oldest shoots or spurs can be removed altogether after flowering, some of the flowered

shoots cut back by about half and a little thinning done. Those grown as wall shrubs should be pruned to produce spurs; cut back the flowering shoots after flowering to leave one or two buds.

Osmanthus Virtually no pruning is necessary, except to cut the oldest shoots down to about half their length occasionally.

Senecio greyi If plants have become gaunt and leggy and if you live in a mild district, you can cut them down hard at the end of this season. This treatment may prove fatal, if the weather turns cold unexpectedly, but as they root so easily from layers or cuttings, pruning is probably not worth the risk involved.

Skimmia Leave well alone and do not prune except occasionally to remove dead and diseased shoots, broken ones and weak or crowded ones.

Spiraea x *arguta* Cut off some of the flowered shoots after flowering, back to strong new or potential new growth. Remove some of the oldest growth to ground level.

Tamarisk (*Tamarix tetrandra*) Little pruning needed but cut back some of the flowered shoots to new ones, to keep the size under control.

Pinching

Although there are some shrubs which flower quite well if left more or less alone, pruning which takes the form of nipping out the tips of the new shoots makes them produce more side-shoots and so become even more flowery. Shrubs which can be treated like this in late spring are fuchsia, cistus and phlomis (Jerusalem sage). When the new shoots are a few centimetres (inches) long, or have about three lots of buds, the tip can be pinched off as far as the next bud or pair of buds down the stem. It delays flowering, of course, but is well worth it. At the same time, if you see any dead growth left over from winter, you can clear it out and leave more room for living stems.

On grape vines, the shoot carrying the flower cluster should be stopped at just above the second leaf beyond the cluster. Any shoots without flowers should have the tip removed at the fourth leaf and minor shoots coming from either of these should be stopped hard, just above the first leaf. This kind of stopping is preferably done when it

Left: *A good heather garden can be a patchwork of colour, especially if the coloured-leaved kinds are grown.* Opposite: *Disbudding peaches. The peach is a prolific bearer of shoots, so unwanted ones are rubbed off to leave the leader, the feeder and the replacement, which are tied in to form an evenly-spaced fan.*

just means taking off the tip. If the shoot has been allowed to grow six or seven leaves long, removal is a much greater shock to the plant and it may retaliate by becoming even more vigorous (see also Pinching, Early Summer).

Disbudding

It may be necessary to do more peach and nectarine disbudding in late spring; the shoots which were left to grow in mid-spring should be tied to the wires as they grow, spaced evenly from one another. If they prove to be crowded, or if other shoots have grown meanwhile, they should be removed. Vines need the same treatment and it is important to tie the retained shoots carefully to the wires. They are brittle and should be tied loosely to start with, gradually tightening the string or raffia until they are close against their supports. Fan-trained, wall-grown Morello cherries are pruned and trained like fan-trained peaches and tying-in of new shoots, as well as removal of unwanted ones, can start now.

Fan-trained, wall-grown apricots seem to fruit much more satisfactorily in temperate climates if only pruned a little, but this leads to bare branches in the centre and fruiting towards the tips. It can be avoided by pinching out most of the new, strong, unwanted shoots from spurs or branches early in late spring, keeping one or two in the centre, to replace the bare oldest shoots which have been removed in winter.

Deadheading

The shrubs which benefit from this and look better as a result, are rhododendron, azalea, pieris, camellia if the dead flowers tend to hang and lilac as it finishes flowering.

Trimming

Some formal hedges are exceedingly quick growing and need a clip over several times a year. If you only trim them once or twice a year they will gradually become taller, bare at the base and will eventually need a ruthless, hard cut. Hedges to trim towards the end of late spring include *Lonicera nitida* (it has tiny round evergreen leaves), gorse, hawthorn, privet and myrobalan (*Prunus cerasifera*). If you are short of time, this trimming can wait until the beginning of early summer without much harm.

The main flowering season for rhododendrons is late spring but it can extend to winter and late summer.

Mulching

Late spring is the time when the soil should be moist, as well as warm; putting on a mulch now, once the ground has been freed from weeds, helps make sure that roots will have a supply of moisture deep down when the hot weather comes. Organic mulches stop the soil from cracking in a drought, encourage worms in the soil and supply nutrients. They can be rotted garden compost, spent hops, leaf-mould, seaweed, rotted, chopped-up young green bracken, which contains a lot of potash, farm manure, spent mushroom compost or peat. Don't be put off by the word 'spent' to describe mushroom compost; it still contains a good deal of food and humus-providing material, which makes it extremely good for ordinary plants. However, if it is being sold in sacks door-to-door, be careful that it does not contain lumps of chalk, otherwise it can wreak havoc on your rhododendrons. Peat is quite safe for plants that like acid soil; the drawback is that it contains very little plant food besides nitrogen and even that is released to plant roots only very slowly.

Mulches should be at least 5cm (2in) thick, spread all over the area which the roots reach; they can spread sideways underground as far as the branches or top growth do above ground. Trees, climbers, and roses can all be mulched, as well as the general run of shrubs; it does no harm to mulch hedges, too, if you have enough material to spare. Plants growing close to walls benefit particularly from mulching; the soil there may already be getting dry, so water first if need be.

Tree fruit is generally given a top dressing in autumn, but if the soil is a 'hot', quick-draining one, a mulch now would be preferable. Straw is better than nothing and will have rotted down by autumn. Water-in an application of hoof and horn meal or sulphate of ammonia before putting it on, otherwise a temporary shortage of nitrogen will occur, while the bacteria get to work on decomposing the straw. Wall-grown vines will give the best crops if mulched heavily, with a 10cm (4in) layer.

Watering

Any plant which grows next to a wall or a fence is not only sheltered from cold, but from rain as well. As it is often facing south or west, the temperature gets hotter than other parts of the garden, so water is at a premium. Wisteria is practically always grown up a house or garden wall and is a very thirsty plant. Lack of water is probably one of the main reasons for lack of flowers on wisterias; the buds simply drop off, as they do from runner beans or sweetpeas, when they are growing in drought conditions. Fan-trained

Wisteria sinensis *is one of the many Chinese plants which grow well in Europe, in most soils and sites.*

peaches grown with a wall backing them must have enough water all the way through the growing season. If they have a feast-or-famine water supply, the fruit drops or splits, or the stones crack.

A good watering with a sprinkler for two or three hours may be necessary every fortnight, or even every week, depending on the weather and soil type, for all plants in this position.

Thinning

The peach, nectarine and apricot thinning started in mid-spring may run on into late spring, depending on the season and district, but it should be possible to finish it early in late spring.

If vines start to flower during the next few weeks, they should be thinned to leave one bunch of embryo fruit to every 30cm (12in) of main stem.

Supporting

Continue to tie in climbing plants, trained tree fruit and wall-grown shrubs as they grow. Rambling roses and clematis in particular will need regular tying if they are to provide their best displays.

Right: *Bark-ringing. Remove a 6-12mm ($\frac{1}{4}$-$\frac{1}{2}$in) wide strip of bark in two half-rings from the trunk of a fruit tree, and cover with grafting wax or insulating tape.*

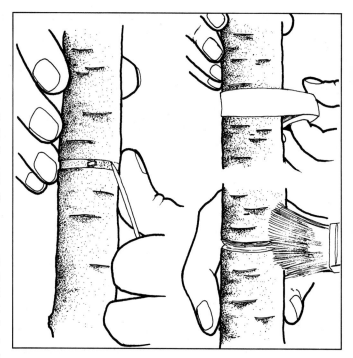

Ringing

If you have any apple trees which are producing many strong new shoots but only a little fruit, you can encourage them to carry blossom and set fruit instead, by removing two half-rings of bark from the trunk. The rings should be 0.6-12cm ($\frac{1}{4}$-$\frac{1}{2}$in) wide, one 2.5cm (1in) above the other. Using a sharp knife, take the bark away down to the wood and then cover the exposed surface with insulating tape while it heals.

Treating pests and diseases

The tree fruits are the main targets for attack in this and the remaining seasons of summer and autumn. Besides such plagues as peach-leaf curl, greenfly, scab, mildew and caterpillars already mentioned, there may also be capsid bug, sawfly caterpillars (which eat the fruitlets), red spider mite, leaf sucker and leaf hopper, pear midge and pear-leaf blister mite, and bacterial canker of cherry and plum liable to infect the shoots, flowers and fruit.

On the ornamentals, peony wilt, clematis wilt, holly-leaf miner, rhododendron bud blast, black spot, mildew and leaf-rolling sawfly on the roses, slugs and fire-blight are possible plagues. The latter can infest tree fruit as well, and grey mould (*Botrytis cinerea*) is a universal fungus disease.

This seems a formidable list of troubles, but it only consists of the most common ones, perhaps a tenth of all those which might infect your plants. However, it is unlikely that what you grow will be affected by even the common kinds all at once, all the way through the growing season. This is the time when they hatch or come to life but it is probable that you will have to deal only with a few of them and—if your plants are well grown and strong—they will be much less severely damaged.

For descriptions of all these and their chemical controls, see the Controls and Treatments section. Remember that cutting out as soon as seen or hand-picking often does all that needs to be done; the birds, too, will help you for a change, as they will have nests full of newly hatched young, demanding food.

General Work

Regular jobs include weeding, compost-heap building, hydrangea blueing and orchard-sward mowing (see Mid-Spring for details of last two).

Plants in flower

Apple (including crab apple), Azalea, Berberis in variety, Buddleia globosa, Ceanothus in variety, Flowering cherry Cotoneaster franchettii, Clematis alpina, C.montana, and some large-flowered hybrids, Cytisus (in variety), Daphne, Deutzia, Eccremocarpus scaber, Fremontodendron, Gorse, Genista, Hawthorn, Heathers (tree), Hebe hulkeana, Horse chestnut, Jew's mallow (kerria), Judas tree (cercis), Kalmia, Kolkwitzia, laburnum, Lilac, Magnolia, Medlar, Mexican orange blossom (Choisya ternata), Mountain ash, Peony (tree), Pieris, Piptanthus, Pyracantha (firethorn), Rhododendron in variety, Rosa banksiae, Spiraea × van houttei, Tamarix tetrandra, Viburnum in variety, Weigela, Wisteria

Early Summer

Early summer is a glorious time in any garden and particularly so where roses and other flowering shrubs are garden features. Large-flowered and cluster-flowered roses, polyanthas, climbers, ramblers, miniatures and the old garden roses provide a tremendous variety of flower colour, fragrance and shape. By making a careful choice it is possible to have roses in flower from late spring until the end of autumn and even then the modern bush roses will often go on producing blooms beyond late autumn. It is not unknown in some gardens to pick the last rose of summer in early winter.

The early-summer-flowering shrubs such as philadelphus (mock orange), rock roses, honeysuckle, clematis, escallonia and weigela overlap the late-spring-flowering sorts and, with sunshine and warmth, the display should draw praise even from the vegetable fanatic, who usually only sees beauty in a well-grown row of spinach or football-sized lettuces.

It is a good season to take time off working in the garden; let the plants get on with growing themselves and wander round the garden to enjoy it and plan some replanting or redesigning. With the roses particularly, you can see if there are any mistakes or gaps during the next few weeks.

Watering begins to be an important job; some feeding will be needed and control of growth by various discreet forms of pruning will still be necessary for shrubs, hedges, fruit and climbers. Some propagation from cuttings will begin to be possible, as new growth becomes established on most plants by now. Pest and disease control becomes less alarming; the onslaughts from the first spring hatches will lose their intensity as insects come to the end of their first—or perhaps only—life-cycle.

At~a~glance diary

Prune: broom (cytisus and genista), ceanothus (spring-flowering), clematis (C. alpina, C. montana) if not done last month, deutzia, lavender cotton (santolina), peony (tree), Spiraea x vanhouttei (S. x arguta if not already done), Tamarix tetrandra

Trim: quick-growing formal hedges; informal hedges

Pinch back: shoot tips of rock roses (cistus), fuchsia, Jerusalem sage (Phlomis fruticosa), young tree lupins

Disbud: apricots, nectarines, peaches, vine; roses for exhibition

Tie-in: tie-in new shoots of fan-trained Morello cherries

Deadhead: azalea, kalmia, lupin (tree), peony (tree), rhododendron

Remove: suckers from roses; plain green shoots from variegated-leaved plants; suckers from framework-grafted trees, suckers from stone fruits

Thin: apple, apricot, peach, pear and nectarine fruits; vine flower clusters if still necessary; vine fruits in early seasons and if early varieties

Water: all wall-grown plants especially wall-grown fruit; wisteria, clematis; newly-planted specimens

Plan: rose gardens, beds and borders

Increase: by soft cuttings, deutzia, fuchsia, hydrangea, Jerusalem sage (Phlomis fruticosa), lavender, lavender cotton (santolina), rock rose (cistus), southernwood (Artemisia abrotanum), spiraea; by seed, any plants which have flowered and set seed

Pests and diseases: as for late spring; also codling moth caterpillars on apples; woolly aphis (American blight) and canker on fruit; canker on roses
mow orchard swards, weed, blue hydrangea, build compost heap, support climbers

Jobs to do

Pruning

The major part of pruning in early summer is taken up with the late-spring-flowering shrubs and some of those flowering early in this season. It may also be necessary to finish off the pruning of the mid-spring bloomers, if they were late flowering because of the weather or an exposed site. Shrubs to prune now are given in the following list.

Broom (Cytisus and Genista) *Cytisus scoparius* and its varieties are shrubs which really need annual pruning, otherwise they get very leggy and sparsely flowered. The flowered sprays should be cut to leave about 2.5cm (1in) of their previous summer's growth; always leave this and do not cut into older growth. Other cytisus species and varieties can also be pruned if flowering has finished, being careful not to prune old wood or unbalance their natural shape.

Most genistas do not need pruning except for the Mount Etna broom (*G. aetnensis*) and one or two others in late summer, and the Spanish gorse (*G. hispanica*) which benefits from a light trim all over with shears after flowering. On the whole, genistas have a tendency to flower themselves to death and there is no need to encourage flowering—rather discourage it.

Ceanothus, spring-flowering. As soon as flowering has finished, the sideshoots on a specimen grown against a wall should be cut back hard, to leave only a few centimetres (1 or 2 inches) of stem. Weak shoots should be removed altogether. Plants growing in the open need not be cut back so hard but if you cut some of the sideshoots by about half the bushes will be denser and the deciduous kinds, in particular, will be less vulnerable to cold.

Clematis Some of the *alpina* and *montana* types may have continued to flower until the end of late spring, so will need dealing with at the beginning of this season. However, it does no great harm if you leave them alone, and *C. alpina* will then produce attractive, fluffy seed-heads, like a cultivated form of old man's beard (see Late Spring for details of pruning).

Kolkwitzia amabilis, *a shrub with charming flowers in late spring, is commonly called the beauty bush.*

Above: *Rose suckers develop from the roots of the stock; they are usually very prickly and have more leaflets. Pull them off: do not use a knife unless it is unavoidable.*

Opposite: *The peach's home country is hot all summer, but with wall protection and a sunny place, the fruit will ripen well in temperate climates.*

Deutzia An easy shrub to prune, as the new growth will be very obvious by now. The flowered shoots at the base should be cleared out and weak shoots removed unless they fill a gap, when they can be left until next spring.

Lavender cotton (santolina) If you did not prune it hard in mid-spring and intend trimming it through the growing season, you can give it the first trim with shears now; the object is to make it bushier and better covered in its silver-grey filigree foliage.

Peony, tree Pruning is not necessary except occasionally, and then only to cut one or two of the oldest stems out completely; tips of shoots infected with grey mould should be removed as soon as seen.

Spiraea The species *S. van houttei* will need its flowered shoots removing at the end of the season, down to where strong new shoots are already growing. The same technique can be applied to *S.* x *arguta* if not pruned in late spring.

Tamarisk (*Tamarix tetrandra*) Prune early this season as described in Late Spring.

Trimming

The quick-growing, formal hedges should be clipped in early summer, if not done in late spring; they provide good, thick hedges, especially the evergreen ones, but they do need quite a lot of attention to maintain their precise shape (see Late Spring for details of hedge cutting).

The informal hedges which have finished flowering can now be trimmed also. However, trimming these is much more like pruning, in that flowered shoots are removed and the new growth thinned a little, if very crowded. If any of these hedges are formed of slow-growing plants, there is no need even to do this, simply cut off dead flower-heads.

Pinching

The removal of the tips of new shoots to just above the first leaf or pair of leaves is called 'pinching'. It is done when the shoots are still young and soft and the tips can literally be pinched between the thumb and first finger nipping them off finally with the nails. It restricts the size of the plant and results in the growth of more side-shoots on the treated stem, so producing more flowers and leaves. Small, quick-growing shrubs, such as rock roses (cistus species), fuchsia, Jerusalem sage (*Phlomis fruticosa*) and young tree lupins benefit from this treatment.

Pinching will also be required for wall-grown vines, removing the tip of a flowerless shoot just above the fourth leaf, and that of a sub-side-shoot above the first leaf. If a shoot has a flower cluster on it, stop it above the second leaf beyond the flowers.

Disbudding

Continue to disbud peaches, nectarines and vines as advised in mid-spring and apricots as advised in late spring.

If you are growing large-flowered or cluster-flowered roses for exhibition, the buds should be thinned during the next two or three weeks to leave only the central one at the end of each main stem.

Tying-in

Continue to tie-in the new shoots of fan-trained Morello cherries as they grow.

Deadheading

As in late spring, rhododendrons and azaleas can be dead-headed and tree lupins will exhaust themselves more quickly if allowed to form seed-pods. Kalmia and tree peony can be similarly treated.

The ornamental japonica will set fruit in a warm summer, quince-like in appearance and flavour.

the roots, are suckers and should be taken off. The leaflets on suckers are generally different in colour and size to those of the true variety.

Suckers on frame-work grafted fruit trees should also be removed; they will be any shoots not growing from the grafts and similarly may result in the tree returning to the original and now unwanted variety. Suckers from the roots of cherries, plums, peaches and all fruits associated with them, should also be dealt with.

Another kind of unwanted shoot is that which has plain green leaves, growing on a shrub or tree with variegated leaves. Sometimes shoots or branches will revert in this way, to the original species; they grow very strongly because they contain much more chlorophyll than the cream- or yellow-variegated form, and eventually take over the plant. Variegated forms are thought to be mutations in some cases, and are not always completely stable, but taking out these rogue shoots as soon as seen is usually sufficient.

Thinning
The wall fruits such as peaches, nectarines and apricots, and vine flower clusters may still need a little thinning if they are late varieties or if the season is cold. Vine fruits may already need thinning, if early (see Mid-Summer for method). Apples and pears can be thinned, if they have set heavily, near the middle of early summer, before the 'June drop' takes place. Thin to leave about three or four fruits to a cluster, removing the centre or 'king' fruit first and then any which are small, damaged or misshapen. After the natural fall, remove any fruits in excess of one or two per cluster.

Watering
Continue to supply all wall-grown plants with water, especially fruit and remember, too, that wisteria and clematis are thirsty plants. If the weather is droughty, newly planted specimens of all kinds will be vulnerable and may even need their top growth sprayed every day as well, if they are evergreen.

Planning
Early summer is a good time to take stock of your rose display and decide whether, and if so where, it needs re-designing and improving. As the large-flowered and cluster-flowered climbers and old shrub roses come into

Removal of unwanted shoots
This is not standard pruning, as it refers to the elimination of very specific growth. In the case of grafted or budded roses, it is the sucker growth from the rootstock which, if left on the plants, will rapidly and easily overcome the named variety. Suckers nearly always come up from soil level, near to a plant, and if the soil is dug away, it will be found growing from a root, usually close to the soil surface.

It should, ideally, be pulled off, to make sure that its point of origin is removed. You can cut it, but because its 'roots' remain, other suckers will sprout from the same point. Some rose stocks sucker particularly badly; those that are least troublesome are the Laxa stocks, said to be hybrid between *Rosa alba* and *R. canina*.

Don't forget that standard roses are budded at the top of the main stem, so that the main stem is in fact stock and any buds on that which sprout, as well as any coming from

flower, you will be able to see the best 'doers', the colour clashes and the weak or badly flowering varieties. By now, you will also be able to pick out the disease-prone kinds; unless you are very partial to them, they are not worth keeping, as they serve as centres of infection.

It is the best time, too, to visit rose nurseries and see how well their stocks are doing in the open, rather than on the bench at a show, where only the best will appear. A visit to your national rose society gardens during the next few weeks could be of great help in obtaining detailed cultural advice, ideas on design of rose gardens and use of roses in a garden, as well as information on new and particularly good varieties.

Increasing

From now until the end of summer it will be possible to take 'soft' tip cuttings of shrubs and climbers. Subjects which can be rooted from such cuttings include: deutzia, fuchsia, hydrangea, Jerusalem sage (phlomis), lavender, lavender cotton (santolina), rock rose (cistus), southern-wood (artemisia) and spiraea. Rooting will be quicker if you can give them a little bottom heat, keeping the compost warm in some way. All can be rooted later in the summer

In this cottage garden, old-fashioned shrub roses and tree peonies mix in delightful profusion, while climbing roses soften the walls of the house and link it with the garden.

from half-ripe cuttings (see Increasing, Late Summer for details of this.)

All tip cuttings should be of the end 7.5cm (3in) or so of new shoots, without flower buds (otherwise they will not root), cut just above a leaf or pair of leaves. Two or three cuttings, stripped of their lowest leaves, are put into 9cm (3½in) pots, to half their length. Firm in and lightly water, then cover with blown-up polythene bags or put into a closed frame and keep warm and shaded until they root.

Many shrubs, trees and climbers which have flowered and set seed can be grown from seed sown now, in an outdoor nursery bed; some will need stratifying first (see Mid-Autumn). Once the seed has got to the stage when it can easily be detached from the plant, it is ready for sowing.

Grafts which were made in early spring may now have grown and taken so well that the wax is acting as a constriction. If it has not cracked, it would be best to remove it.

Softwood cuttings of roses, taken as shown in early summer, are quite as likely to root as hardwood cuttings.

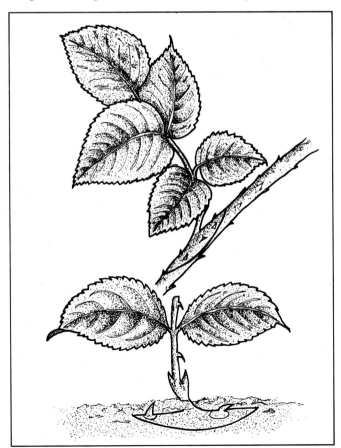

Treating pests and diseases

In addition to the troubles listed in Late Spring, there may be an infestation of codling moth caterpillars, which feed on the pips and the flesh at the centre of apples. Damage can be considerable and the only real answer is to spray; the birds do not seem to be able to get at the small caterpillars before they go into the fruit and other predatory insects appear to be non-existent.

Roses can still be infected by such plagues as black spot, mildew, greenfly, leaf-rolling sawfly grubs, leaf-cutting bees and chafer beetles. Scab, mildew, aphis, particularly woolly aphis (American blight) and canker, as well as codling moth, can infest fruit. For chemical controls, see the section on Controls and Treatments of plant troubles at the end of the book.

General work

The tasks are much what they were in the latter parts of spring. Continue to mow orchard swards, weed, blue hydrangeas, build the compost heap and support climbers as required (see Mid- and Late Spring for details).

Plants in flower

Broom (Cytisus scoparius and varieties, genista and Spanish broom), Buddleia globosa, Ceanothus, Clematis, Cotoneaster, Deutzia, Eccremocarpus, Escallonia, Fremontodendron, Fuchsia, Hawthorn, Hebe, Honeysuckle, Jasmine (summer-flowering), Jerusalem sage, Kalmia, Kolkwitzia, Laburnum, Lilac species, Lupin (tree), Magnolia, Mexican orange blossom (Choisya ternata), Mountain ash, Peony, Philadelphus (mock orange, syringa), Potentilla, Pyracantha (firethorn), Rhododendron (late), rock rose (cistus), Roses, Solanum, Tulip tree (liriodendron), Viburnum, Weigela, Wisteria

Mid-Summer

Early summer and mid-summer are the main seasons for large-flowered, cluster-flowered and shrub roses, old and new. The latter flower in mid-summer and some kinds will continue to flower for the rest of the summer, following their first heavy flush of blooms. Some of the climbers are repeat-flowering, too.

Mid-summer is also the time when there is a new wave of shrub-blooming; after the spring flowers, the fuchsias, hydrangeas, hypericums, hebes, hibiscus and many other plants which prefer summer warmth come into their own and decorate the garden all over again. Fruit, such as cherries, mulberries and the very earliest pears and apples will begin to ripen. Towards the end of mid-summer in sheltered places, picking of the early varieties of peaches, apricots and nectarines can start.

Much of the month's work consists of routine jobs but pruning takes on a new pattern, as the restricted fruit trees begin to need their summer cutting, cherries require their annual pruning and the hybrid tea and floribunda roses need treatment after flowering. There will still be a little pruning of flowering shrubs, left over from early summer, and some hedges may need trimming.

If you have plants which you would like to increase, mid-summer is the time to start taking what are known as semi-ripe cuttings from shrubs, and to start budding roses. It is also a good time to order new stock from the nurseries, to make sure that it arrives when you want it to, in the autumn.

At~a~glance diary

Prune: Buddleia globosa, deutzia, escallonia, kolkwitzia, lavender cotton (santolina), philadelphus (mock orange), Senecio greyi, weigela; summer-prune restricted pears, fan-trained and bush cherry

Trim: fast-growing formal hedges; informal flowering hedges

Deadhead: rock rose (cistus), roses, rue, Senecio greyi

Thin: fig, grape, fruits

Feed: camellia, peony (tree), roses; plants growing in light soil

Water: newly planted specimens, wall-grown plants; all in drought

Order: all plants to be delivered from specialist nurseries

Increase: roses by budding; various shrubs and climbers from semi-ripe cuttings, tip cuttings, layering

Pests and diseases: as for early summer; in addition red plum maggot, silver leaf of plums and other plants, tortrix caterpillar on apple and pear, rose rust, earwig on clematis and other plants

Routine work: weed, mow orchard sward, build compost heap, blue hydrangea, remove suckers and plain green shoots, tie-in climbers

Jobs to do

Pruning

For the flowering shrubs, there is not a great deal of pruning during mid-summer, possibly a few left over from late spring and the few that have flowered last season. However, even if a shrub does not need formal pruning every year, it nearly always accumulates dead shoots; just clearing these out completely seems to give many a new lease of life. Anything which flowers or grows poorly, including weak shoots, diseased ones and broken or crowded growth, should be cut off completely to its point of origin.

Buddleia globosa When the flowers have finished, a little of the oldest growth can be removed, cutting these stems back by about a quarter of their length.

Deutzia If not dealt with already, this should be pruned

Rosa Mundi, *or Rosa gallica* Versicolor, *one of the oldest shrub roses, can be traced back to the Middle Ages.*

early in mid-summer, as detailed in Early Summer.

Escallonia These shrubs can have their flowered shoots pruned off as soon as flowering has finished, back to a strong new shoot. Those kinds with long arching shoots can become rather untidy and need this pruning every year; others can be missed occasionally. If grown as wall shrubs, they will need hard cutting to leave only a few centimetres (inches) of the flowered shoot, so that they remain compact.

Kolkwitzia (beauty bush) Prune off the flowered stems and cut out one or two of the oldest main stems to ground level occasionally, to encourage new growth from the base.

Lavender cotton Trim all over with shears towards the end of mid-summer.

Philadelphus (mock orange blossom) Cut the flowered sprays back to strong new growth and thin out some of the new growth if getting too tall or crowded.

Senecio greyi If it has been allowed to flower, clip immediately after flowering with shears, to give it plenty of time to renew itself before winter.

Weigela Like deutzia and philadelphus, easily pruned by removal of flowered growth as soon as flowering has

For those who like their apples crisp and juicy, Granny Smith is ideal for dessert, and stores late into winter.

finished, to allow space for the new shoots already growing.

Summer-pruning of espalier or cordon-trained apples can sometimes be started at the end of mid-summer, if the season is dry, but is normally begun in the first week of late summer. Pear growth matures a little earlier than apples, and does have to be treated late in mid-summer (for details see Pruning, Late Summer).

The pruning of fan-trained sweet cherries grown against walls consists of cutting the new side-shoots back to just above the fifth or sixth leaf in late mid-summer, with further pruning following in early autumn. Leading shoots which were bent over last autumn, should be cut back to a weak side-shoot.

Bush sweet-cherry trees grown in the open need little pruning, beyond removing dead, diseased, broken, crowded or weak shoots and occasional cutting back of the main branches or leaders to keep within bounds. This should be done as soon as the crop is picked.

Trimming

The fast-growing formal hedges will probably need a second clip early in mid-summer, depending on when they had their first one; informal flowering hedges will need cutting if they have finished blooming (see Early Summer for details).

Deadheading

Remove the dead blooms of rock roses (cistus) as they form seed easily and then flower less. If you prefer the foliage of rue to its mustard-yellow flowers, these will need cutting off and *Senecio greyi*, if allowed to flower, should at least have the dead flower clusters clipped off. Large-flowered, cluster-flowered, climbing and rambling roses should all be deadheaded, unless their hips are wanted for decoration or seed. Large-flowered should be cut back by about half their length; cluster-flowered, climbers and ramblers should have the complete flower cluster cut off. All cuts should be made just above a leaf with an outward-pointing bud in its axil.

Thinning

Figs should be thinned round about mid-summer; they are fertile trees and in warm countries ripen heavy crops, in successive stages. However, in temperate climates the small, hard figs which are present in autumn will never ripen and only hinder the production of more fruit. As soon as these can be seen to be developing in mid-summer, they should be removed. The result is that more embryo fruit forms but remains dormant until the following growing season, when it starts to swell in late spring and is large enough to ripen by late summer.

Grapes will need thinning early in this season, if not already done, starting when the fruit is about the size of a sweetpea seed. Remove the smallest berries and the innermost ones first; then, starting at the bottom of the bunch, remove at least half the remainder, until the shoulders are reached, where very few should be removed. Thinning should be done in two stages, before and after stoning, as with peaches, and sufficient space should be left to accommodate the berries comfortably when they are fully grown—about 2.5cm (1in) diameter, depending on variety. Use sharp, pointed scissors to cut out the unwanted berries.

Feeding

This is a good season to feed one or two spring-flowering shrubs which begin to form their flower-buds for next spring now, on this year's new shoots. They include camellia and tree peony, which is a notoriously greedy plant.

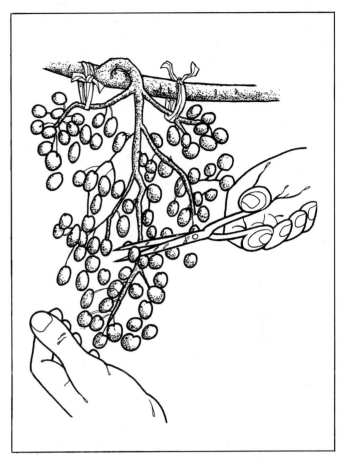

Grapes set a great number of berries and in order to be well-sized they must be thinned to remove more than half.

A general compound fertilizer with a high proportion of potash can be used, potash alone as sulphate of potash at the rate of 15-30g per sq m (½-1oz per sq yd) or ash formed as a result of burning wood—about 150g per sq m (5oz per sq yd). Roses can have a second feed after their first flowering, and if your soil is light, all will be grateful for a feed with a balanced compound. Watering-in of any fertilizer application at this time is advisable.

Watering

Be very careful to make sure plants do not go short of moisture now. Drought in summer followed by winter waterlogging is death to many woody plants but if kept in good health in summer, they can withstand winter weather better. Container-grown specimens, newly planted, are very much at risk, as are all wall-grown plants, especially the fruits. Shortage of water now results in their dropping the whole crop on the ground.

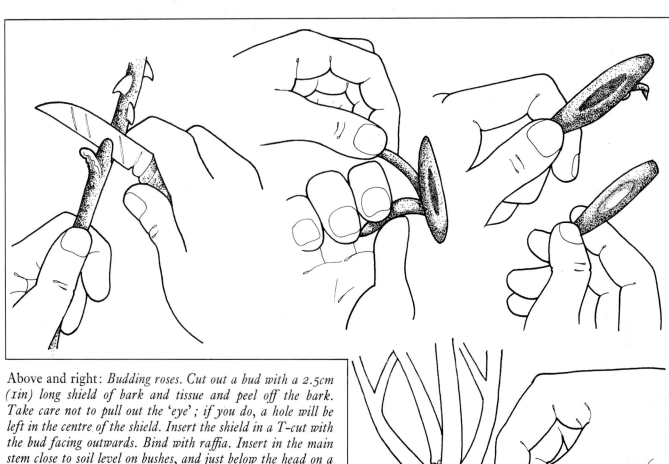

Above and right: *Budding roses. Cut out a bud with a 2.5cm (1in) long shield of bark and tissue and peel off the bark. Take care not to pull out the 'eye'; if you do, a hole will be left in the centre of the shield. Insert the shield in a T-cut with the bud facing outwards. Bind with raffia. Insert in the main stem close to soil level on bushes, and just below the head on a standard.* Opposite: *A perfect large-flowered (hybrid tea) rose.*

Ordering

Mid-summer is a good time to get ahead in the queue for plant delivery; ordering what you need now from the nurseries will ensure that your plants arrive when you want them to, weather permitting. You will not be so far down the list that you have to wait till mid-winter.

Increasing

If you want to increase the number of your rose varieties, do it by budding in mid-summer. Basically the method consists of making a T-shaped cut in the bark of the rose stem to be budded, and then slipping into this a bud, backed by a sliver of woody tissue, of the new variety. You can take the buds from new shoots of the selected variety, about half-way up the stem, and use as stock either a variety you no longer want or one of the special rootstocks used for roses: *Rosa canina* (the wild dog-rose), or *R.* x *laxa*, which you have to buy. These are themselves grown from hardwood cuttings taken in mid-autumn.

In mid-summer, some shoots of shrubs and climbers will be sufficiently mature to supply semi-ripe cuttings (see Late Summer for details). You can also take tip cuttings of the plants listed in Early Summer and the layering method of increase is still possible for many plants.

Treating pests and diseases

Another spray for codling moth caterpillars will be necessary, as well as one for red plum maggot, which can decimate plums in mid and late summer. Silver leaf on plums and other fruit can be cut out now. Woolly aphis (American blight) may be a considerable problem and tortrix caterpillars on apples and pears can do a lot of damage without being noticed until picking time. Red spider mite and mildew are still other potential menaces on fruit. Black spot, rose rust and mildew on roses will need treatment, and earwigs on clematis and other plants will be in evidence. The remaining pests mentioned in early summer should be much less troublesome.

Honeysuckles will flower in succession from early summer until autumn, depending on variety; they need little care.

Plants in flower

Abelia grandflora, Broom (cytisus and genista in variety), Spanish broom (Spartium junceum), Buddleia davidii in variety, Ceanothus, Clematis, Cotoneaster, Daisy bush (Olearia haastii), Deutzia, Eccremocarpus scaber, Escallonia, Fremontodendron Fuchsia, Heather (ericas), Hebe, Honeysuckle, Hydrangea, Hypericum, Indigofera gerardiana, Jasmine (summer flowering), Jerusalem sage (Phlomis fruticosa), Kalmia, Koelreutaria, Lavender, Lavender cotton (santolina), Leycesteria formosa, Lupin (tree), Magnolia, Philadelphus (mock orange, syringa), Rhododendron, Rock rose (cistus), Roses, Russian vine (Polygonum baldschuanicum), Senecio greyi, Solanum, Spiraea, Tamarisk (Tamarix pentandra) Tulip tree (liriodendron), Yucca

Harvest

Apple (early varieties), Cherry, Mulberry, Pear (early varieties)

Late Summer

Most activity in late summer is related to fruit crops, rather than ornamentals; you will find that much of your time is taken up with picking and harvesting various kinds of tree fruits. A good deal of the pruning needed is associated with the fruits, too, if you are growing the restricted forms, such as fans, espaliers and cordons.

There will still be a little shrub pruning; late summer is the season for trimming formal hedges, both deciduous and evergreen. The fast-growing kinds may be needing their third clip and some deadheading and sucker removal will still also be necessary.

Semi-ripe cuttings of many shrubs, including climbers, can be taken now. At this time of the year, they have the best chance of rooting and surviving, while conditions are still warm and there is plenty of time for them to build up a good root system and top growth. Other methods of increase include budding early in the season and layering.

The pest and disease war will begin to peter out and though you may still be fighting off mildew, earwigs and woolly aphis, the remaining plant troubles will definitely be diminishing. Many pests will have come to the end of their life-cycle and will be looking for suitable places in which to winter. Birds and wasps will be problems on the fruit, particularly the wall-grown crops.

At~a~glance diary

Prepare the soil for: planting outdoors in early autumn — e.g. evergreens, and/or winter-flowering shrubs and trees

Prune: wisteria; restricted forms of apple, pear; bush plum, greengage; bush cherry, fan-trained Morello cherry

Trim: formal, deciduous and evergreen hedges: examples are beech, cypress, holly, hornbeam, privet, yew; informal flowering hedges, provided the flowering has finished

Deadhead: Buddleia davidii, lavender, lavender cotton, roses, rock rose (cistus), rue, Senecio greyi, yucca

Feed: camellia, peony (tree), roses

Pot: rooted cuttings from mid-summer

Increase: roses by budding; various shrubs by layering or by semi-ripe cuttings

Pests and diseases: codling moth caterpillars (third spray), tortrix caterpillars and woolly aphis on apples; red plum maggot (second spray); black spot, mildew and rust on roses; red spider mite, mildew, earwigs, birds and wasps generally; put corrugated cardboard or sacking bands round trunks of apple trees

Jobs to do

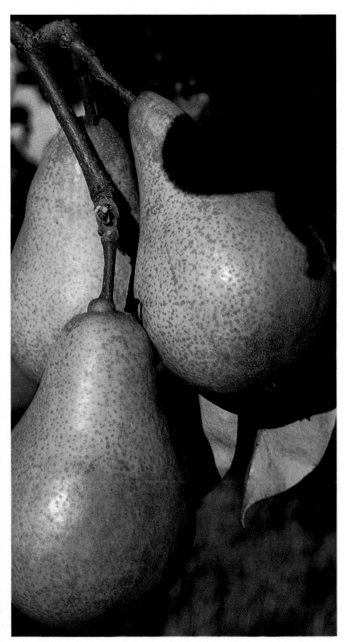

Preparing the soil for planting
Early autumn is one of the best seasons for planting evergreens, conifers in particular, and so, some time in late summer, the soil of the chosen site should be dug and rotted organic matter mixed in as in the preparations for planting detailed in Mid-Autumn. If the soil is dry, a thorough watering a day or two beforehand will be necessary. Evergreen planting does, of course, include evergreen hedges, so preparation could mean digging out trenches, not merely individual planting sites.

Pruning
Virtually no shrub and climber pruning will be needed in late summer, except to wisteria. This is done to encourage more flowering, but you can leave it alone and simply prune it to fit the space available in winter. For summer pruning wisteria, all this year's new side-shoots are cut back to leave a length of about 30cm (12in), or about six leaves. The leading shoots should be cut back similarly.

Summer pruning of both apples and pears grown as cordons or espaliers is as follows. When the new side-shoots have matured to the stage at which the bark is light brown for about half the length of the stem, the rest gradually changing colour until it is a fresh green at the tip, the shoot should be cut to leave a length of about 15 or 17.5cm (6 or 7in). This applies to sub-side-shoots as well. Shoots which are not sufficiently mature should be left until they are, and then pruned. After the middle of early autumn it is too late to summer-prune, however, and they should be left alone.

It is important that the shoots are pruned at the right stage of maturity; too soon, and the buds which should have turned into fruit buds instead produce new shoots which do not mature by winter and are then killed. Too late, and the shoot does not bud up to form fruit buds. The first week of early summer is often the best time for the majority of trees and gardens but warm conditions can mean pruning

Pear Beurré Clairgeau is an early-flowering culinary variety which is ready for picking in mid-autumn.

Left: *Summer-prune cordon and espalier apples and pears by cutting the new growth just above a leaf, to leave 15-17cm (6-7in) of stem.* *Below:* Cobaea scandens, *the cup-and-saucer plant, is a half-hardy climber for the greenhouse or warm garden.*

much earlier, during the latter half of mid-summer and cold ones will put pruning back to the second or third week of late summer.

Bush-grown plums may also have what little pruning is necessary done after the fruit has been picked. Infection by silver-leaf fungus is much less likely at this time; it infects through wounds and is most troublesome in winter, so that pruning then can be disastrous. Plums fruit on two-year-old shoots and on naturally formed spurs, so all that has to be done is to encourage some new side-shoots to form every year. Too much pruning results in a great deal of strong vegetative growth, so perhaps only a quarter of the season's new side-shoots should be cut back to four or five leaves or cut out completely. If there are any strong, new shoots growing straight upwards from the lower branches, these should have the tips removed; in time they can be used to replace the drooping branches which become unfruitful. Keep the tree clear of crowded, diseased or weak growth.

Bush forms of sweet cherries can be pruned after the fruit has been picked (see Pruning, Mid-Summer, for details). Fan-trained Morello cherries should be pruned after picking by cutting the fruited shoots off, back to a stub, on which is the replacement shoot.

Trimming

Some time in late summer the formal deciduous and evergreen hedges can be given the annual clip; you could leave the deciduous kinds until winter but it is much less pleasant then and you may be prevented by the weather from doing it until too late.

You can make the job easier, if doing it by hand, by using really good quality, sharp, shears. If you have great lengths of hedges, a powered hedge-trimmer is a very worthwhile investment; it is now possible to obtain battery-driven models. When choosing one, make sure the weight is not going to be overpowering after half-an-hour or so of use; also, make sure the grip is completely comfortable and the right size for your hands. This applies to shears as well. Handles which are too thick are very tiring and rapidly produce blisters.

As soon as you start having to stretch up to cut, stand on a tripod ladder, steps or stool. Start from the bottom

Plants for Hedges

Plants for formal hedges
Beech
Berberis
Box
Cotoneaster simonsii
Cypress
Escallonia
Euonymus japonicus
Hawthorn
Hebe
Holly
Hornbeam
Laurustinus
Laurel
Spotted Laurel (aucuba)
Lonicera nitida
Privet
Pyracantha (firethorn)
Tamarix
Yew

Plants for informal hedges
Berberis
Cotoneaster
Currant, flowering
Daisy bush (olearia)
Deutzia
Escallonia
Forsythia
Fuchsia
Gorse
Hawthorn
Heather
Hebe
Hydrangea
Japonica
Lavender
Lavender cotton (santolina)
Philadelphus
Pyracantha (firethorn)
Rhododendron

Roses
Spiraea
Tamarix
Viburnum
Weigela

Roses for hedges
Rosa moyesii
Rosa rugosa
    Blanc Double de Coubert
    Frau Dagmar Hastrup
    F. J. Grootendoorst
    Roseraie de l'Hay
    Sarah van Fleet
    Schneezwerg
Frühlingsgold
Frühlingsmorgen
Pemberton Musk roses
Penzance Briars
Zephirine Drouhin

when cutting the sides of the hedge and use a line stretched along the top to prevent the appearance of scallops on the horizontal edge. If, however, you want scallops or castellations, use two lines to mark both the dips and the tops. Hedges of laurel and bay are better cut with secateurs, otherwise the leaves are badly damaged.

Although most hedges can be dealt with once a year, in late summer, there are exceptions, as given in the accompanying table. This also details the method of cutting hedges after the second winter from planting, to ensure that they have leaves down to ground level.

Deadheading
Plants to deadhead through late summer include rue, lavender cotton (santolina), *Senecio greyi* if not already done, rock rose (cistus) and roses in general. New subjects to treat will include lavender, yucca and *Buddleia davidii* varieties.

Magnolia denudata, or the Yulan lily, whose home is China, bursts into fragrant flower in spring.

Feeding

It is still worthwhile giving a potash-high fertilizer to camellias, tree peonies and roses as mentioned in Mid-Summer, as early as possible this season.

Potting

Some, if not all, of the shrub cuttings taken in mid-summer will have rooted by now and will need larger pots and a good potting compost. The size of pot depends on the amount of root produced and should be large enough for the roots not to be cramped. The young plants can be kept outdoors quite safely and will need regular watering.

Increasing

Rose budding may be possible early this season, provided the bark still lifts easily (see Increasing, Mid-Summer, for details). Any increase by the layering method also needs to be done early, so that the layers are well rooted by autumn.

Late summer is a good time to make semi-ripe cuttings

Opposite: Those exotic flowers of the South Seas, the hibiscus, have some hardy relatives in the shape of the shrubby H. syriacus. *Blue Bird is one variety, flowering in late summer.*
Right: Before planting a semi-ripe cutting, trim the heel. Plant the cuttings round the rim of the pot to about half their length. Cover the pot with plastic to keep the atmosphere at the level of warmth and moisture the cuttings need.

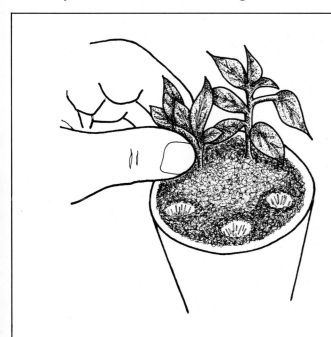

of shrubs and climbers. These cuttings should be about 5-17.5cm (2-7in) long, made from this year's shoots. The shoot will have begun to mature so that the bark is starting to brown and harden from the base of the shoot but the tip will still be green and soft. The cutting is made in the usual way (see Increasing, Early Summer).

Treating pests and diseases
Troubles to contend with now will probably be earwigs eating the petals and leaves of clematis, mildew, which causes most trouble in early autumn, especially after dry summers, woolly aphis on apples and pears and birds and wasps on fruit of all kinds. Wall-grown fruit can be protected with netting against birds and jam jars full of sweet liquid will sidetrack the wasps from the fruit.

The St John's Worts all have yellow saucer flowers with long stamens in summer; Hypericum x inodorum *Elstead mixes red berries with the flowers in late summer.*

Late summer is the time to put corrugated cardboard or sacking collars, about 10-15cm (3-6in) wide, round the trunks of apple trees, just below the main branches. These collars provide places for codling caterpillars to pupate and their removal in autumn ensures a good deal of control and reduction of damage to next year's crop.

Other pests and diseases will be as for mid-summer but by now the need for spraying should virtually have finished.

General work
Continue to water, build the compost heap and remove suckers and plain green shoots. Hydrangeas will be flowering and should not need any more blueing treatment for the time being; weeding will be much less, unless the summer is wet. Climbing plants will have grown to their limit and may now only need to have their ties reinforced after summer gales. Orchard swards need not be mown if time is short.

Plants in flower

Abelia grandiflora, Buddleia, Campsis Mme Galen, Ceanothus, Ceratostigma willmottianum, Clematis, Daisy bush (Olearia haastii), Eccremocarpus, Escallonia, Eucryphia, Fremontodendron, Fuchsia, Gorse, Heather (Calluna vulgaris and ericas, including E. cinerea) Hebe, Hibiscus, Honeysuckle, Hydrangea, Hypericum, Indigofera gerardiana, Jasmine (summer-flowering), Koelreuteria paniculata, Lavender, Leycesteria formosa (himalayan honeysuckle), Magnolia, Mallow (tree), Potentilla, Rock rose (cistus), Roses, Russian vine (Polygonum baldschuanicum), Solanum, Spanish gorse (Spartium junceum), Spiraea, Tamarix pentandra, Wisteria, Yucca

Harvest

Apple, cherry, Greengage, Mulberry, Nectarine, Peach, Pear, Plum

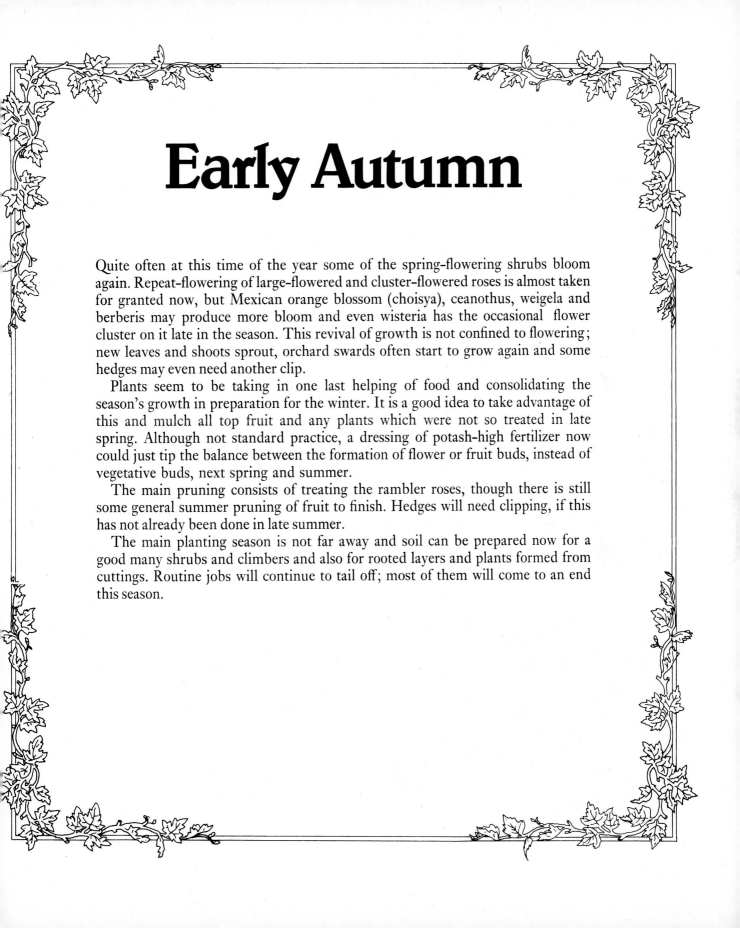

Early Autumn

Quite often at this time of the year some of the spring-flowering shrubs bloom again. Repeat-flowering of large-flowered and cluster-flowered roses is almost taken for granted now, but Mexican orange blossom (choisya), ceanothus, weigela and berberis may produce more bloom and even wisteria has the occasional flower cluster on it late in the season. This revival of growth is not confined to flowering; new leaves and shoots sprout, orchard swards often start to grow again and some hedges may even need another clip.

Plants seem to be taking in one last helping of food and consolidating the season's growth in preparation for the winter. It is a good idea to take advantage of this and mulch all top fruit and any plants which were not so treated in late spring. Although not standard practice, a dressing of potash-high fertilizer now could just tip the balance between the formation of flower or fruit buds, instead of vegetative buds, next spring and summer.

The main pruning consists of treating the rambler roses, though there is still some general summer pruning of fruit to finish. Hedges will need clipping, if this has not already been done in late summer.

The main planting season is not far away and soil can be prepared now for a good many shrubs and climbers and also for rooted layers and plants formed from cuttings. Routine jobs will continue to tail off; most of them will come to an end this season.

At~a~glance diary

Prepare the soil for: planting

Plant: evergreen and evergrey plants, except the least hardy kinds; winter-flowering plants; rooted layers and plants grown from cuttings

Prune: rambler roses; fan-trained sweet cherries and peaches; plums; finish summer-pruning restricted apples and pears

Trim: formal deciduous and evergreen hedges if not done already

Deadhead: Buddleia davidii, hebe, lavender, roses, rue; hydrangea in warm districts

Feed: with potash-high fertilizer

Mulch: shrubs, climbers, top fruit that has cropped, rambler and climbing roses, hedges

Water: if weather dry

Increase: evergreens and deciduous plants from semi-ripe cuttings

Pests and diseases: birds, wasps, mildew, especially on vine and roses, black spot on roses, earwigs; apply greasebands to fruit trees

Routine work: weed, finish compost-heap making, remove suckers and plain green shoots, blue hydrangeas

Jobs to do

Preparing the soil for planting
Ideally, soil should be dug, manured, fed and cleared of weeds about four or five weeks before planting but it is often difficult to get the timing right, taking into account delivery from the nursery and the fickleness of the weather. The object of this early preparation is to ensure that the additions to the soil become broken up and absorbed to some extent by the time the plants are put in, so that they can make use of the added goodness at once. Then their establishment is much quicker and your chances of success are much greater (see Mid-Autumn for details).

Planting
Early autumn has been found to be the best time to plant most winter-flowering and evergreen or evergrey shrubs and

A garden with a superbly-kept lawn, planted with conifers, will be a pleasure to look at in summer and winter.

trees. The least hardy kinds can be left until mid- or late spring if time is short now or if your district is a cold one. Sometimes the autumn is dry and warm and, if so, the planting sites should be thoroughly watered a day or two before planting, as well as immediately after preparation. Make sure that all the plants are well firmed in and securely attached to supporting stakes before the big autumn gales start (see Late Autumn for details of planting).

Pruning

Roses, particularly the ramblers, are one of the main groups of plants to need treatment in early autumn; they flower profusely on the previous season's new growth and can be encouraged to produce good long stems if the flowered shoots are cut right away to ground level. The job can be simplified by untying both flowered and new shoots and placing them full length on the ground; weak and stunted growth should be pruned off as well. The new canes are then retied to their supports, well spaced out.

Fan-trained sweet cherries grown against walls should have the side-shoots, which were cut to five or six leaves in

Left: Potentilla fruticosa *is a shrub whose flowers vary in colour from primrose to deep gold.*

Below: *Planting a conifer. Plants supplied by mail-order should have the sacking removed from the root-ball and the ball planted intact, with soil filled in over it.*

mid-summer, further cut to three or four now. If the leading shoots have grown too tall, they should not be pruned, but bent over and tied down, when they should produce side-shoots.

If the peach harvest has finished, the trees can be pruned in the way described in detail later, under Pruning, Early Winter.

Plums which have finished cropping can be pruned by the methods recommended in Late Summer and will be all the better for being cleared, not only of their fruit, but of unnecessary shoots and twigs.

The summer pruning of restricted apples and pears should be finished early in autumn; at the same time, if any secondary shoots have grown after the earlier summer pruning, these should be completely removed. They will never mature satisfactorily and the tips will be damaged by cold, which can lead to fungus infection setting in.

As far as the shrubs and climbers are concerned, both flowering and foliage kinds, no pruning is required in early autumn unless it was missed in late summer and some catching up has to be done.

Right: *Solanum crispum Glasnevin is a slightly tender climber, which flowers intermittently all through summer.*

Below: *A temporary screen should protect the conifer from wind, and the foliage should be sprayed daily from planting time until the plant is well established.*

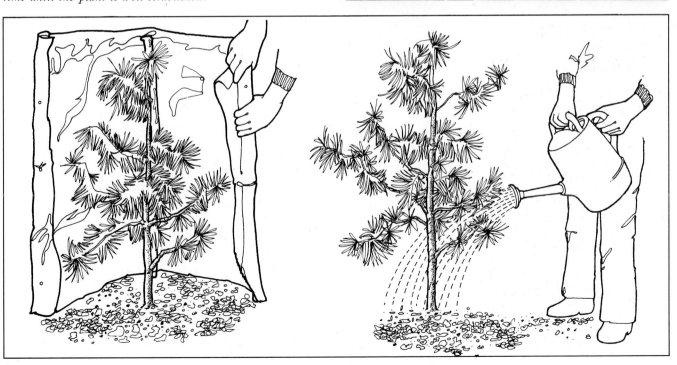

Trimming

There is still time, early this season, to trim formal deciduous and evergreen hedges, if they were not done in late summer. In fact, some are best left until now; these include bay, elaeagnus, laurel and spotted laurel (aucuba).

Deadheading

Plants to deadhead include *Buddleia davidii* varieties, late-flowering lavenders, all types of roses where necessary, rue if still flowering, and hebe. In warm districts the flower-heads can be taken off hydrangeas, but otherwise they provide a little protection from cold for the buds just below them which will flower next year.

Feeding

Although feeding plants is not generally recommended at this time of the year, it is the leaf-and-shoot-producing nutrient, nitrogen, that could result in trouble. Its application would encourage rapid, 'soft' growth, easily burnt by frost and cold wind. Phosphorus and potassium, however, will make the roots stronger and mature the shoot growth without increasing it, thus making it harder and more resistant to low temperatures. A compound fertilizer with a small nitrogen content could therefore be applied now and would be particularly beneficial to plants growing in sandy or shingly soil.

Mulching

By now the compost heap started in spring should have rotted down to the brown, crumbly substance which does so much good to the soil structure. It can be used as a mulch for shrubs, climbers, top fruit that has been picked and pruned if necessary, rambling and climbing roses and hedges. Privet has a bad reputation for taking all the goodness out of the soil and herbaceous plants growing close to privet hedges grow poorly because of this, so it pays to mulch such hedges well now, besides feeding them in spring.

Watering

There are some autumns when the idea of artificial watering is that season's joke but, equally, there can be others which make the Gobi Desert look wet! Whatever the weather, keep an eye on the wall plants, the evergreens and the new plants so that they never become parched.

Increasing

Semi-ripe cuttings of deciduous shrubs and climbers can still be rooted this season, preferably early rather than late.

It is a good time to increase conifers, such as cypresses, juniper, cedar and larch from heel cuttings and other evergreens, for which semi-ripe cuttings are used (see Late Summer). Heel cuttings are much used for the conifers, and may only be 5 or 7.5cm (2 or 3in) long. The shoot is pulled off, not cut, so that a sliver of bark and older wood is attached to the shoot; this 'heel' is trimmed of its ragged edges and the cutting then put into a moist sandy compost, or moist silver sand alone. If the latter is used, the cuttings must be potted as soon as rooted, as there is no food in the sand.

Opposite: *Dessert plums take a lot of beating as to flavour if eaten when freshly picked and still warm from the sun.* Below: *The shrubby veronicas, now called hebes, carry their flowers in spikes, long or short. Autumn Glory will flower until early winter in mild seasons.*

In their native Mediterranean regions figs will set at least two crops of fruit a year. In colder climates only one is possible in sheltered places outdoors. In order to obtain this, the small hard fruits present in mid-summer should be rubbed off the shoots.

Some conifers, such as spruce (picea) and fir (abies), have a good deal of resin in them. Dipping the ends of the cuttings in hot water for a few minutes prevents this resin from forming a callus over the end of the cutting, which would prevent rooting.

After potting, the cuttings can go into a shaded cold frame.

Treating pests and diseases
Birds and slugs will still be damaging fruits a good deal and mildew on vines and roses can be very troublesome in early autumn. Black spot on roses, and earwigs generally, are other current plagues. Female winter moths and March moths will be preparing to lay eggs on branches of apples, pears and plums and can be prevented by putting grease-bands round the trunks of the trees (and supporting stakes) about 60-90cm (2-3ft) above the ground. Grease-bands can be bought ready for use from garden shops.

General work
It is a good idea to get on top of weeds in rose beds, in beds round specimen plants and those growing beneath wall or fence-trained plants and hedges, in early autumn. Otherwise, by next spring, they can easily have got completely out of hand. Orchard swards may need mowing, depending on the weather. The second compost heap or heaps will be nearly finished. There will be few, if any, suckers and plain green shoots to remove and climbing plants will have finished their upward growth. Hydrangeas should be given one more blueing treatment.

Harvesting
The apple and pear harvest will be in full swing during early and mid-autumn. If you are in doubt about the maturity of a fruit, test it by holding it in the palm of your hand and pushing it gently upwards. The stalk should come away easily, but if it needs a good tug, leave the crop for a few more days. A colour change from green to yellow is another indication and a third, if you can bear to cut a fruit open, is the colour of the pips. They should be dark brown when the fruit is ripe. Other fruits to harvest include: apricot, damson, fig, greengage, nectarine, peach, plum and vine.

Plants in flower
Berberis, Buddleia davidii, Campsis Mme Galen, Caryopteris, Ceanothus, Ceratostigma Clematis, Fremontodendron, Fuchsia, Gorse, Heather (Calluna vulgaris and ericas including E. cinerea), Hebe, Hibiscus, Honeysuckle, Hydrangea, Hypericum, Indigofera, Jasmine (summer-flowering), Leycesteria formosa, Magnolia grandiflora, Mexican orange blossom (choisya), Potentilla, Roses, Russian vine (Polygonum baldschuanicum), Solanum, Sorbaria, Spanish gorse (Spartium junceum), Spirea, Tamarix pentandra, Weigela, Wisteria

Harvest
Apple, Apricot, Damson, Fig, Greengage, Nectarine, Peach, Pear, Plum, Vine

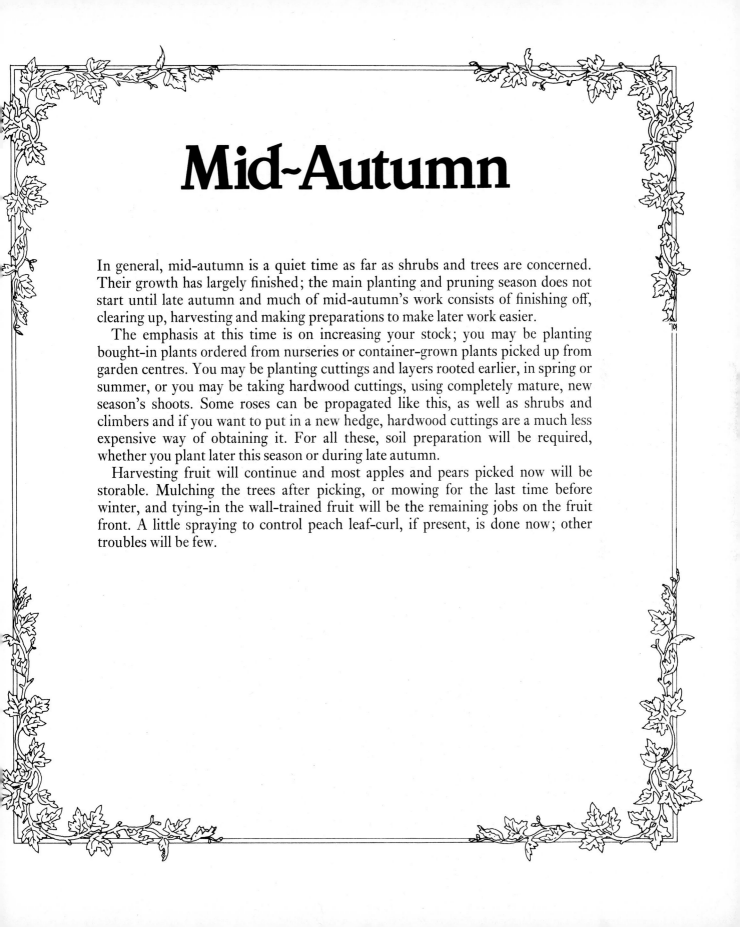

Mid~Autumn

In general, mid-autumn is a quiet time as far as shrubs and trees are concerned. Their growth has largely finished; the main planting and pruning season does not start until late autumn and much of mid-autumn's work consists of finishing off, clearing up, harvesting and making preparations to make later work easier.

The emphasis at this time is on increasing your stock; you may be planting bought-in plants ordered from nurseries or container-grown plants picked up from garden centres. You may be planting cuttings and layers rooted earlier, in spring or summer, or you may be taking hardwood cuttings, using completely mature, new season's shoots. Some roses can be propagated like this, as well as shrubs and climbers and if you want to put in a new hedge, hardwood cuttings are a much less expensive way of obtaining it. For all these, soil preparation will be required, whether you plant later this season or during late autumn.

Harvesting fruit will continue and most apples and pears picked now will be storable. Mulching the trees after picking, or mowing for the last time before winter, and tying-in the wall-trained fruit will be the remaining jobs on the fruit front. A little spraying to control peach leaf-curl, if present, is done now; other troubles will be few.

At~a~glance diary

Prepare the soil for: planting at the beginning of early spring —e.g., deciduous shrubs, climbers, ornamental and fruit trees

Plant: deciduous shrubs and trees; evergreens if not done; rooted layers and cuttings taken in spring and early mid-summer, rooted vine eyes

Prune: rambler roses, potentilla, summer jasmine

Mulch: all shrubs, climbers, fruit trees (even if the crop is not yet picked), ornamental trees

Deadhead: hebe, hydrangea, roses

Sweep up: leaves to form a heap to rot down into leafmould (do not use diseased or leathery leaves)

Increase: by hardwood cuttings rambling and climbing roses, shrub roses, some species and some cluster-flowered roses, deciduous and evergreen shrubs in variety; by seed, trees

Pests and diseases: peach leaf-curl, black spot, mildew, birds

Routine work: weed, complete compost heap, water new plants, mow orchard sward for the last time

Store: apple, pear, quince, in a dry, cool, frost-proof place, safe from vermin

Jobs to do

Preparing the soil for planting

The woody plants are the most permanent part of the garden, and the most costly, so it pays to take steps to avoid death of the plants shortly after planting. It is essential to supply the roots with as favourable conditions for re-growth as possible. Late autumn is the best time, as far as weather is concerned, for planting roses, deciduous shrubs, climbers and trees; advance soil preparation in mid-autumn (except for light soils) will result in food, aeration and drainage being at their best by the time the plants are put in.

Unless your soil is a well-drained, deep, fertile loam, it will be the better for the addition of rotted organic matter. Use any of the materials suggested in Late Spring for mulches: farm manure, garden compost, leafmould, spent hops or spent mushroom compost. It must be rotted, because unrotted material may remain in the state in which it was added to the soil for many months. Heavy soils can have about 3kg per sq m (7lb per sq yd) mixed in, medium soils about 4½kg (10lb per sq yd) and sandy, shingly or chalky soils need about 6½-8½kg per sq m (15-18lb per sq yd).

In the case of these light soils, preparation should be left until a few days before planting, otherwise the organic matter added will be absorbed too quickly by the soil flora and fauna and be less useful.

Soil should be dug two spits deep, keeping the topsoil separate from the lower spit. The bottom of the second spit should be forked up, mixing organic matter with it at the same time. Planting holes should be at least 60 × 60cm (2 × 2ft) square; as the soil is replaced, organic matter is mixed with it, and the whole left to settle until planting.

If you are planting at the beginning of late autumn, bonemeal should be added about a week before the end of mid-autumn, at the rate of about two large handfuls per sq m (sq yd); mix it into the top spit with a fork. Bonemeal contains phosphorus, the mineral plant food so much needed by developing roots.

When preparing the site, large stones and weeds should

The colour of the leaves of many shrubs and trees in autumn can be spectacular and is a point to remember when choosing varieties. Acer nikoense is a slow-growing tree to 12m (40ft), with particularly brilliant leaf colour.

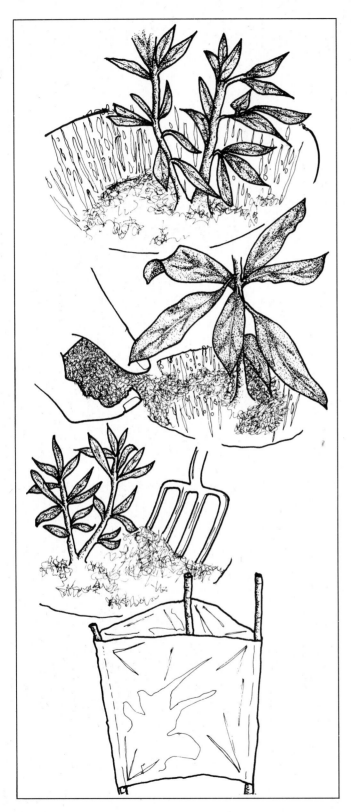

be cleared away; roots of perennial weeds should be dug out completely. Bindweed, ground-elder, couch grass and horsetail will be a particular nuisance later if not thoroughly dealt with now.

You may want to grow rhododendrons, azaleas and other plants that love acid soil in a neutral-to-alkaline soil, but although you can create pockets of acid soil for them, in time these will become alkaline, due to soil drainage and rain. It is a constant fight to grow plants under these conditions and, in any case, they never look quite right in their surroundings. On the whole, it is better not to go against the grain: try, instead, some of the many attractive lime-tolerant trees and shrubs available: clematis, coton-easter, buddleia, box, ceanothus, cistus, forsythia, fuchsia, laburnum, syringa and viburnum, for example.

Planting

It is not too late to plant evergreens, except in cold districts, though even in the warmer ones they should go in as soon as possible. Deciduous shrubs and trees can also be planted now, as well, though it is better to wait until leaf fall, and rooted layers and cuttings, including vine eyes, will be ready (see Late Autumn for details of planting).

Pruning

Rambler roses can be pruned in mid-autumn if not so treated in early autumn.

If potentilla was not pruned in spring, and it has some rather old, non-flowering growth, this growth, which may be several stems, can be removed to ground level. Such pruning need only be done every few years. Potentilla is one of the few shrubs which naturally has a brown cambium layer, rather than a green one, below the bark, so do not assume that it is dead because of this.

Summer jasmine produces a lot of annual growth which gets much tangled; flowering falls off unless one or two of the oldest shoots are cut off to soil level in mid-autumn and the remainder thinned by cutting shoots back here and there. In cold districts this can be left until spring.

Left: *Planting rhododendrons. Plant so that the root-ball is undisturbed, with the soil mark on the stem at the same level as the soil surface; crumble soil on to and around the root-ball to fill the hole; rake or lightly fork the surface of the firmed-down soil and give temporary protection from the wind or cold.*
Right: *A corner of a rock garden with an attractively mixed planting of rhododendrons and dwarf shrubs. These include a Japanese maple and an upright juniper.*

Mulching
All fruit trees can be mulched now, even if a crop is not yet picked, as later mulching will not be made use of to the same extent. Keep the mulch clear of trunks, otherwise mice and voles nest in it and feed on the bark of the trees during the winter months.

Deadheading
Roses will still need removal of finished blooms; hebe flower spikes are better removed and so are hydrangea flowerheads if the garden is warm and the buds below the flower heads do not need their protection from cold.

Sweeping up
In the last week or so of this season, the leaves will start to fall; rather than let them smother the ground-cover shrubs and provide a place for pests and disease to winter, they should be collected up into a heap to rot down into leaf-mould. Leaves which should not be added are the leathery kinds, usually evergreens, and those infected with diseases such as scab, black spot and mildew; these are better burnt.

Increasing
Mid-autumn is the best season for increasing woody plants from hardwood cuttings. These consist of the end 22.5-

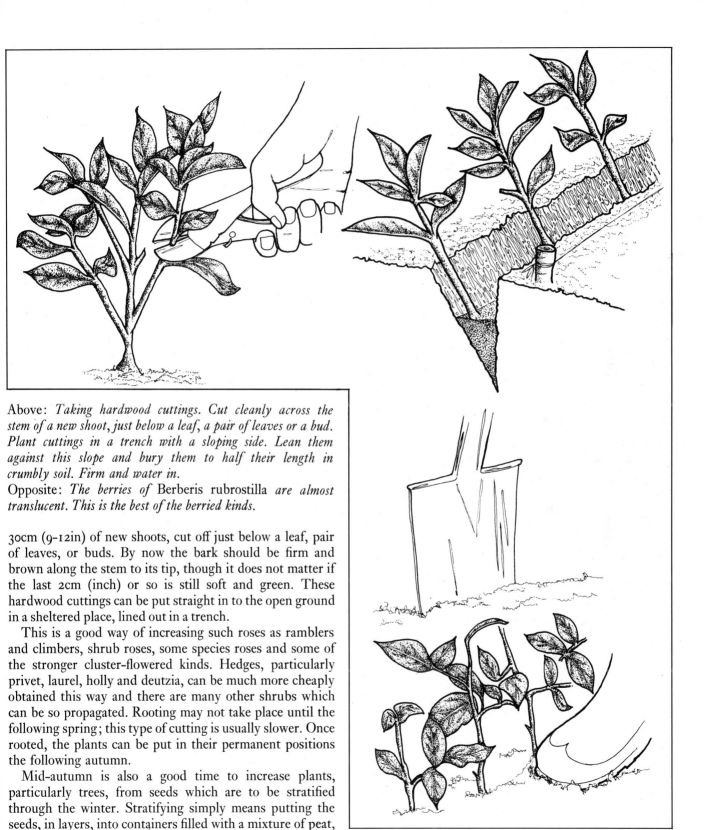

Above: *Taking hardwood cuttings. Cut cleanly across the stem of a new shoot, just below a leaf, a pair of leaves or a bud. Plant cuttings in a trench with a sloping side. Lean them against this slope and bury them to half their length in crumbly soil. Firm and water in.*
Opposite: *The berries of* Berberis rubrostilla *are almost translucent. This is the best of the berried kinds.*

30cm (9-12in) of new shoots, cut off just below a leaf, pair of leaves, or buds. By now the bark should be firm and brown along the stem to its tip, though it does not matter if the last 2cm (inch) or so is still soft and green. These hardwood cuttings can be put straight in to the open ground in a sheltered place, lined out in a trench.

This is a good way of increasing such roses as ramblers and climbers, shrub roses, some species roses and some of the stronger cluster-flowered kinds. Hedges, particularly privet, laurel, holly and deutzia, can be much more cheaply obtained this way and there are many other shrubs which can be so propagated. Rooting may not take place until the following spring; this type of cutting is usually slower. Once rooted, the plants can be put in their permanent positions the following autumn.

Mid-autumn is also a good time to increase plants, particularly trees, from seeds which are to be stratified through the winter. Stratifying simply means putting the seeds, in layers, into containers filled with a mixture of peat, coarse sand or a mixture of the two. The containers are then plunged (sunk up to the rim) in a bed or border close to a north-facing wall or fence. They should be covered with close-mesh netting to prevent mice getting at the seeds. Seeds treated like this are those with hard coats; roses (the whole hip is buried), hawthorn, peach and plum stones and holly are examples. They may need to stay there until spring only, or a year and a half, and the more they are frozen the better.

Treating pests and diseases
Be sure to spray for peach-leaf curl, just as the leaves are about to fall (see Controls and Treatments section for fungicide required). Black spot and mildew may still be present on roses; birds may be menacing fruit.

General work
There may be a little weeding left to do. The compost heap will be completed now and can be covered for the winter;

In Mexico, Choisya ternata *is a common shrub; its fragrant flowers justify its English name of Mexican Orange Blossom.*

in a dry autumn newly planted specimens should be kept well watered. Give the orchard sward a last mow.

Storing
Certain varities of apples, pears and quinces can be stored through the winter until late spring, but they must be in a frostproof place and they must be safe from mice and rats. Sheds and garages are not necessarily frostproof in bad winters and storing the fruit in wooden boxes or on slatted racks invites trouble. Thick, wooden chests, with slatted shelving inside, lagged against the cold with fibreglass wool or several layers of sacking should be safe, but a cellar, unheated attic or spare room is better.

Apples, pears and quinces should be stored separately from one another; they can be placed four or five in a clear plastic bag, stored singly, or wrapped in oiled paper. If stored in a pile in a box or chest, all must be quite free from injury or disease, otherwise trouble spreads rapidly, and you do not want to turn out several hundredweights of apples every few weeks to see whether the bottom ones are rotting.

Plants in flower

Caryopteris, Ceanothus, Ceratostigma, Cherry (autumn-flowering, Prunus subhirtella autumnalis), Clematis, Fatsia, Fuchsia (shelter), Gorse, Heather, (Calluna vulgaris and ericas, including E. carnea in variety), Hebe, Honeysuckle, Hypericum, Hydrangea, Mexican orange blossom (choisya), Roses, Russian vine (Polygonum baldschuanicum), Strawberry tree (Arbutus unedo), Witch hazel (Hamamelis virginiana)

Harvest

Apple (late varieties), Fig, Grape, Pear (late varieties), Quince, Sloe

Late Autumn

Your main job in late autumn will be planting. Although it can, in theory, be done at any time during winter, late autumn or early winter are best. Roses, deciduous shrubs, trees, climbers, tree fruits, vines and hedges can all go in now; the hardier evergreens can also be planted but are less likely to survive in very cold winters. Staking and pruning will be part of the process.

Pruning the tree fruits can be started towards the end of late autumn, once the leaves are completely off. Wall-grown fruits can be re-tied after spacing and possibly cutting if necessary and some shrubs and climbers may need surgical treatment. Another form of late-autumn pruning is root pruning, done to fruit which is obstinate about cropping.

The end of late autumn is also a good time to cover vulnerable plants with netting to protect them against birds, cold or wind, and to make sure that all those needing supports are securely attached before gales, snow and heavy rain start. Apart from these, there are various odd jobs to do, which are mostly a matter of finishing off; these include picking the remaining fruit, sweeping up leaves and taking hardwood cuttings.

At~a~glance diary

Prepare the soil for: planting at the beginning of winter all subjects except evergreen and tender plants

Plant: deciduous shrubs and trees, climbers, roses, hedges, tree fruits, the hardier evergreens

Transplant: deciduous shrubs and ornamental trees, climbers, roses, hedging plants, fruit trees, and the least tender evergreens

Prune: tree fruits, rambler roses; root prune unfruitful tree fruits

Mulch: finish mulching; give tender plants extra deep mulch at least 15 cm (6in) deep above crowns and the side root area

Sweep up: leaves

Protect: tree fruits and some ornamentals against bud pecking by birds; newly planted and young plants against cold and wind

Increase: by hardwood cuttings taken early this season, rambling and climbing roses, shrub roses, some species and some cluster-flowered roses, deciduous and evergreen shrubs in variety; by stratified seed trees, shrubs and roses; clematis by layering

Routine work: finish weeding, store fruit; examine supports and ties and repair where necessary

Jobs to do

Preparing the soil for planting

You may not be able to plant until the end of this season, or even sometime during early winter, but soil will need digging and manuring a few weeks in advance, as detailed in Mid-Autumn. If it is very wet, due to early autumn rains, leave the soil alone, especially clay soil, which can become severely compacted if trampled on while wet. It will also be very heavy work.

Planting

The reason for planting at this time of the year is that the soil is still relatively warm from the summer, the air temperature has not fallen really low and the plants are not completely dormant, but still capable of growing new roots.

At this time of the year, it should be possible to put in plants directly they arrive when bought by mail-order from a nursery. If, however, conditions are cold and the soil frozen or waterlogged, they can be left in their wrappings for a few days, provided the roots have moist peat, compost, or sacking round them. If the weather looks like being difficult for some time, as it may do in winter, they should be heeled in to a shallow trench in a sheltered place for the time being.

If you are using container-grown plants from a garden centre or bare-rooted plants from the gardening department of a general store, you can, of course, choose your time for buying, so that it coincides with good weather.

Spacing of plants is very important. You need to know the spread, almost more than the height, of a mature tree

Left: *The winter jasmine,* Jasminum nudiflorum, *is a weakly climbing shrub in flower from late autumn to spring.*
Below: *Stratifying seeds. Tree and shrub seeds are sown in a peat/sand mixture, protected from mice with netting.*

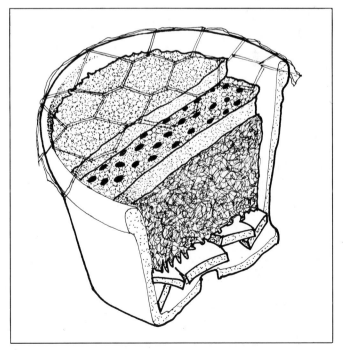

Above: Viburnum x burkwoodii *is a heavily fragrant spring-flowering shrub ; height is about 2.4m (8ft).*
Opposite: Williams' Bon Chrétien, *or the Bartlett pear, is good to eat raw, and also bottles and cooks well.*

Fruit Tree Spacing

Apple,	bush	2.4-4.5m (8-15ft)
	cordon	60cm (2ft)
	espalier	3.6m (12ft)
Apricot, fan		3-7.2m (10-24ft)
Cherry,	sweet bush	4.5m (15ft)
	fan	4.5m (15ft)
	Morello	4.2-6m (14-20ft)
Damson, bush		4.5-5.4m (15-18ft)
Fig, fan		2.4m (8ft)
Grapevine, single rod		1.2-1.5m (4-5ft)
Greengage, bush		3-4.5m (10-15ft)
Medlar, bush		4.2-4.8m (14-16ft)
Mulberry, bush		9m (30ft)
Peach (nectarine)	fan	4.2m (14ft)
	bush	4.5-6m (15-20ft)
Pear,	bush	3.6-5.4m (12-18ft)
	cordon	90cm (3ft)
	espalier	3.6m (12ft)
Plum, bush		4.5-5.4m (15-18ft)
Quince, bush		3.6m (12ft)

or shrub (see table of ornamental shrubs and trees for these dimensions). In nearly every case, not enough space is allowed, and the plant has cramped growth, flowers and leafs less well than it might and becomes much more prone to infection and pest epidemics. If proper spacing means rather large gaps for some years, you can fill them up with annuals, herbaceous plants or quick-growing shrubs like the tree lupin, rock rose (cistus) or broom. For spacing of fruit, see the list.

There is one major rule about planting, which really amounts to the difference between success and failure: always make sure that the roots are spread out to their fullest extent in the planting hole. Never plant so that the roots are in a doubled-up handful; it is tantamount to strangling them, and even if the unfortunate plant survives, it never grows well.

Dig out a hole which is more than wide enough and deep enough. Make a shallow mound in the centre and set the plant in the hole so that the roots spread naturally over and down the mound. Crumble good topsoil or a compost mixture in over the roots, shaking the plant gently every now and then so that all the crevices are filled and firming as the hole fills. Firm by treading, starting at the perimeter of the hole; firming from the centre outwards will result in the tips of the roots pointing upwards rather than downwards. Do not tread on the roots unless they have soil on them.

If any roots are torn or broken off with a jagged edge or are much longer than the others, cut them cleanly below the damage. Plants produce two sorts of roots; anchoring kinds which are long and stout and fibrous ones which are fine and short and which are the feeding roots. It is these that the plant will need most urgently; anchoring can come later. This is why you should plant firmly and provide a stake and/or shelter from wind while the plants are young and establishing.

Planting should generally be at the same level as in the nursery or container, shown by a soil mark on the stem, but fuchsias can be about 5cm (2in) lower if planted now and will then survive the winter with a heaped-up protective mulch over them. Roses must always be planted so that the grafting bump is above the soil.

Some plants will arrive from the nursery with the root-ball wrapped in sacking or other material, having been lifted with the soil because they have formed a tightly packed mass of fine roots. Rhododendrons, azaleas and many conifers are examples. When planting, the roots should be left undisturbed and the soil-ball planted intact, with a little topsoil crumbled over the top.

If a stake is needed, put it in position in the hole before planting, to avoid later injury to the roots and, if you are dealing with standards, use a stake which reaches to just below the main head of branches. Bush tree fruits can have shorter stakes.

After planting, water the plant in and rake the topsoil gently to produce a rough rather than a smooth surface, for better drainage and aeration. It is advisable to keep the soil round the plants clear of grass or weeds, in a circle about 60cm (24in) in diameter for two or three years, to avoid competition for water and food while the plants establish.

Unless there are any very strong or ungainly shoots on the plants, there is no need to do any initial pruning at this time except to the roses. The large-flowered and cluster-

Opposite: *Planting trees. Spread the roots out, and position the tree on a shallow mound in the centre of the hole. Line up the soil mark with the soil level, using a board, and stake. Fill in soil; support tree with a suitable tie.*

Below: *The berries of* Symphoricarpos albus, *the snowberry, last a long time as they are not at all popular with birds.*

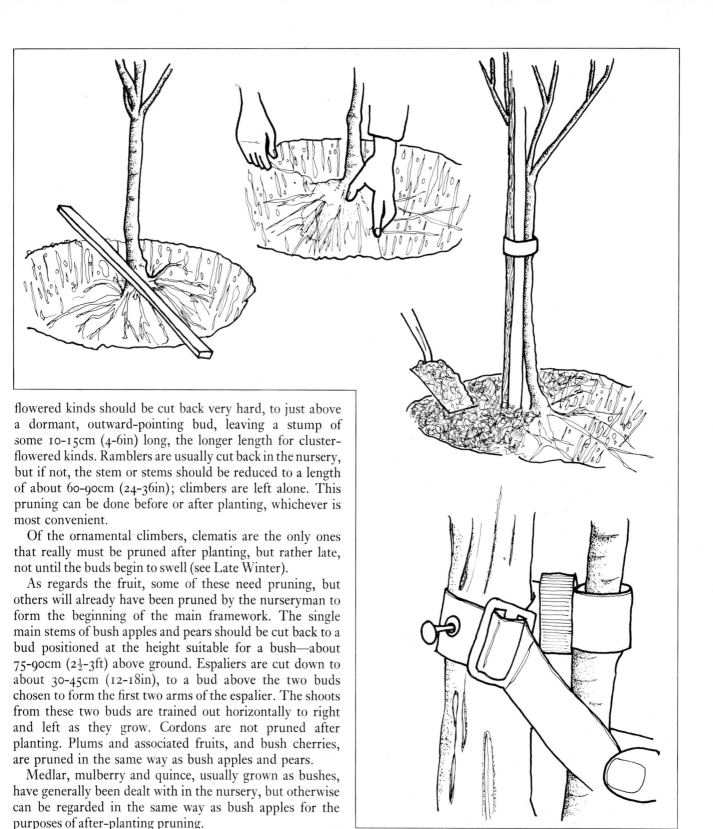

flowered kinds should be cut back very hard, to just above a dormant, outward-pointing bud, leaving a stump of some 10-15cm (4-6in) long, the longer length for cluster-flowered kinds. Ramblers are usually cut back in the nursery, but if not, the stem or stems should be reduced to a length of about 60-90cm (24-36in); climbers are left alone. This pruning can be done before or after planting, whichever is most convenient.

Of the ornamental climbers, clematis are the only ones that really must be pruned after planting, but rather late, not until the buds begin to swell (see Late Winter).

As regards the fruit, some of these need pruning, but others will already have been pruned by the nurseryman to form the beginning of the main framework. The single main stems of bush apples and pears should be cut back to a bud positioned at the height suitable for a bush—about 75-90cm (2½-3ft) above ground. Espaliers are cut down to about 30-45cm (12-18in), to a bud above the two buds chosen to form the first two arms of the espalier. The shoots from these two buds are trained out horizontally to right and left as they grow. Cordons are not pruned after planting. Plums and associated fruits, and bush cherries, are pruned in the same way as bush apples and pears.

Medlar, mulberry and quince, usually grown as bushes, have generally been dealt with in the nursery, but otherwise can be regarded in the same way as bush apples for the purposes of after-planting pruning.

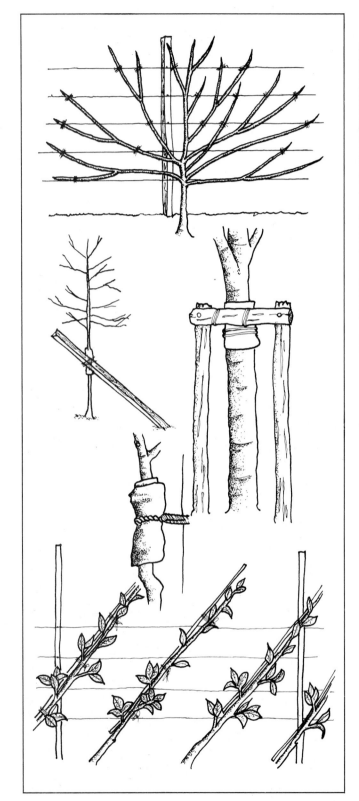

Group A	Group B	Group C
Clip several times a year; cut leading shoots lightly until height required is reached, then cut at that height always. Cut sides hard always. Cherry plum (*Prunus cerasifera*), hawthorn, gorse, *Lonicera nitida*, privet	Cut once a year in late summer; cut leaders lightly until height required is reached, then cut hard. Cut sides hard always. *Berberis buxifolia nana*, beech, cotoneaster, all cypresses, escallonia *Euonymus japonicus*, hebe, holly, hornbeam, juniper, laurustinus, *Osmanthus delavayi*, pyracantha, snowberry, tamarix, *Thuja plicata*, yew	Clip once a year, in early autumn. Cut sides fairly hard, and leaders as advised for Groups A and B Bay, elaeagnus, laurel, spotted laurel (aucuba)

Berberis darwinii and *B. stenophylla* : treat as Group B, but in late spring

Left: *Types of tree support vary according to the shape of the tree for which they are required. Illustrated here are the wire support for a fan-trained tree, types of wooden stake to support a standard, and the support for cordons.*

Fan-trained wall-grown fruit, such as peach and Morello cherry, are cut down to about 30cm (12in) above the grafting union, and the growth from the two topmost buds about 20cm (8in) above the union used to form the first ribs of the fan. These are tied down gradually as they grow to a final angle of 45°. Figs usually have the basic fan formed in the nursery and need not be pruned immediately.

Grape vines should be cut down to leave two or three dormant buds, which may mean reducing the stem to about 15-45cm (6-18in). However, if they are planted later than the end of mid-winter, do not prune, otherwise they will 'bleed' and this will weaken them. The leading shoot which then grows strongly from the top bud in summer is used to form the fruiting 'rod' and will also need to be cut hard in late autumn by as much as two-thirds of its length.

Newly planted hedges will need some degree of cutting back directly after planting, but if planted in late winter or early spring, should not be so treated. They should be left to grow during the summer and then cut back in late autumn as directed for those planted in autumn and the early part of winter.

The informal hedges, with the exception of the brooms and the evergreens, should be cut down hard to leave about 30cm (12in) of stem. This will ensure good bushy growth right from the base.

In the second winter after planting, Groups B and C are treated as in the first, but Group A should be cut back hard so as to remove half the growth produced in the summer.

Transplanting
As with planting, this is a good season to transplant woody plants. The method is much the same; when lifting the plants, try to keep the roots as intact as possible and re-plant as quickly as possible. This means having the holes dug ready beforehand. Keep a good ball of soil round the roots. If the plants have to be out of the ground for a while, cover the roots with moist peat or wet sacking as soon as dug up. If they become dry and then wither, especially the rootlets, their chances of establishing and developing successfully are much decreased.

Pruning
Towards the end of late autumn, after finishing any mulching left over from mid-autumn, you can start to prune the bush-tree fruit and finish the pruning of the restricted forms, such as cordons, fans and espaliers, started in summer (see Early Winter for details). Rambler roses can still be pruned, if there has not been time to do it so far (see Early Autumn).

Late autumn is a suitable time to root-prune fruit trees to encourage them to fruit. Some trees, in a very fertile, deep soil, become too strong and put all their energy into producing shoots instead of fruit. One way to overcome this is to dig a trench round the tree about 30cm (12in) deep and 45-60cm (18-24in) wide, so that the roots can be seen and loosened. The smaller and finer ones are tied back out of the way and the thickest sawn off; then the fine roots are replaced in position and the trench filled in with fine soil. With established trees, this should be done in two stages, half one autumn or winter and half the next year.

Mulching
Any mulching not done or finished in mid-autumn should be completed early this season; on romneyas, eccremo-carpus and fuchsias it will serve as a frost protection if 15cm (6in) or more deep.

Sweeping up
This is the season for collecting leaves. All will make good leafmould, except the leathery and/or evergreen kinds.

Those infected with fungus disease, such as black spot and scab, should be burnt and it is particularly important to sweep these up so that fungus spores do not overwinter on them.

Protection
Although it is difficult to believe, bullfinches and other birds are quite likely to start pecking out the fruit buds of gooseberries, greengages, damsons, plums, pears, cherries

The spindle-tree is a plant of North European hedgerows, but its bright berries make it gardenworthy.

and apples at any time from late autumn through winter to spring, so protective netting, webbing, or bird-repellent sprays should be put on now before they start.

Increasing
Hardwood cuttings can still be taken early in late autumn and seeds stratified. If you have clematis you would like to propagate, you can do so by layering, at any time from now until spring. Use a shoot which was produced the spring before last, i.e., about 18 months old, close to the ground. Plunge a 15cm (6in) pot full of cutting compost into the soil to its rim, bend the shoot to form a 'U' into the pot so that it is buried in compost and keep it in place with a wire hook or wooden peg. By the following autumn it will have rooted and can be detached and planted.

General work
There may be a little weeding to do; the summer spraying of pests and diseases is over and winter spraying, if it is necessary, need not be started until pruning is finished. Securing of ties, stakes and supporting trellises should be done before gales start in earnest. The last late varieties of apples and pears can be put into store.

Plants in flower
Cherry (autumn-flowering, Prunus subhirtella autumnalis), Fatsia, Heather (Erica carnea varieties), Hebe, Jasmine (winter-flowering, Jasminum nudiflorum), Laurustinus, Mahonia Charity, Roses, Strawberry tree (Arbutus unedo), Viburnum farreri, Witch hazel (Hamamelis virginiana)

Harvest
Apple, Grape (last), Medlar, Pear

Below: Apples can be stored in single layers, in shallow trays stacked so that air can circulate between them.

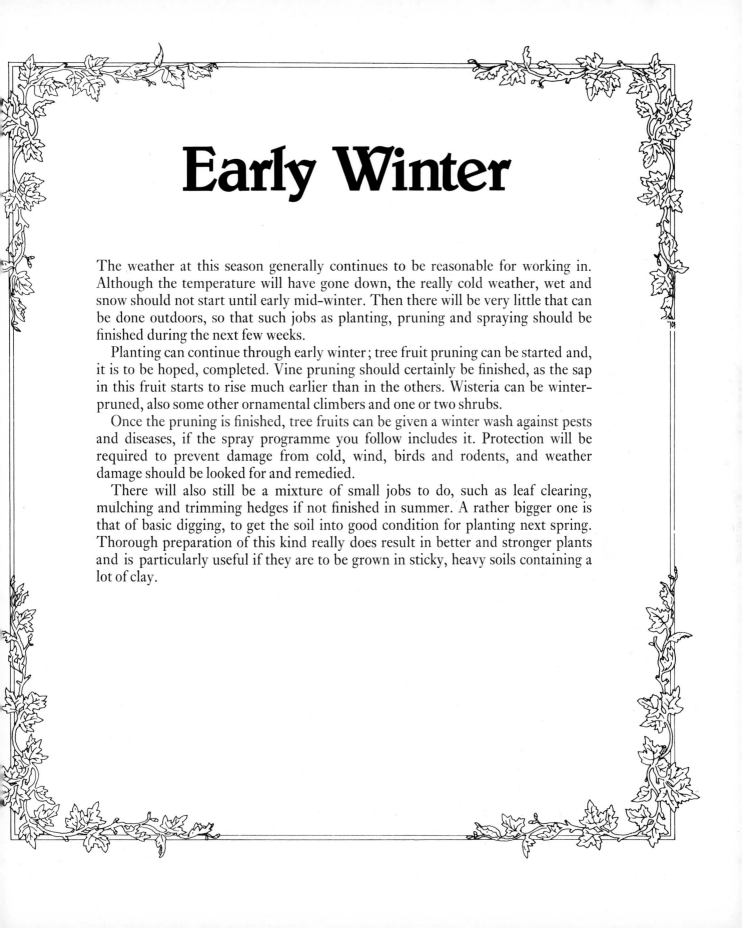

Early Winter

The weather at this season generally continues to be reasonable for working in. Although the temperature will have gone down, the really cold weather, wet and snow should not start until early mid-winter. Then there will be very little that can be done outdoors, so that such jobs as planting, pruning and spraying should be finished during the next few weeks.

Planting can continue through early winter; tree fruit pruning can be started and, it is to be hoped, completed. Vine pruning should certainly be finished, as the sap in this fruit starts to rise much earlier than in the others. Wisteria can be winter-pruned, also some other ornamental climbers and one or two shrubs.

Once the pruning is finished, tree fruits can be given a winter wash against pests and diseases, if the spray programme you follow includes it. Protection will be required to prevent damage from cold, wind, birds and rodents, and weather damage should be looked for and remedied.

There will also still be a mixture of small jobs to do, such as leaf clearing, mulching and trimming hedges if not finished in summer. A rather bigger one is that of basic digging, to get the soil into good condition for planting next spring. Thorough preparation of this kind really does result in better and stronger plants and is particularly useful if they are to be grown in sticky, heavy soils containing a lot of clay.

At~a~glance diary

Prepare the soil for: planting for double digging (digging to two spades' depth)

Plant: hardy deciduous shrubs and ornamental trees, climbers, roses, hedging plants, fruit trees (not evergreens or grey-leaved shrubs)

Prune ornamentals: large-flowered and cluster-flowered roses, if rather leggy, shrub roses if necessary, campsis, overgrown or crowded honeysuckle, summer jasmine, wisteria

Prune fruit: apple, apricot, Morello cherry, fig, medlar, mulberry, nectarine, peach, pear, quince, vine

Save: prunings from apples and pears for framework grafting

Protect: against birds; protect the following against wind, cold, winter weather. Abelia x grandiflora, campsis, ceanothus, Clematis armandii, eccremocarpus, escallonia, fremontodendron, fuchsia, hebe, hibiscus, summer jasmine, Mexican orange blossom (choisya), phlomis, piptanthus, privet, rock rose (cistus), romneya, Senecio greyi, solanum, yucca

Sweep up: leaves

Increase: by hardwood cuttings, vine

Pests and diseases: black spot and rust on roses; spray apples, pears, cherries, plums, greengages and other tree fruits with tar-oil winter wash to control over-wintering eggs of aphids and apple sucker, and adult scale insects; spray vines with sulphur to control scale insects, and with soft soap for mealy bug

Jobs to do

Preparing the soil for planting

Early winter is usually a good time to do some basic digging of previously uncultivated soil or to improve badly structured soils. These include those which are markedly quick-draining, such as chalky, sandy and shingly soils or heavy and water-retentive ones, such as sticky clay, peat and silt. To grow plants successfully in these soils, it is advisable to dig them a few months in advance of planting, mixing in soil improvers, such as rotted organic matter, coarse sand or grit, peat, and lime if very acid. The soil should be dug to a depth of two spades, the bottom of the hole or trench forked up and mixed with rotted manure, garden compost or similar material and the soil, together with the soil improvers, returned. The top spit should be kept separate from the second, so that they can be returned in order, and unmixed.

If lime is thought to be necessary, to break up a heavy soil or to decrease extreme acidity, it should be mixed in some weeks after adding organic matter, otherwise a chemical reaction occurs which results in loss of nutrients from the soil.

Once the soil has been roughly dug, it can be left until early spring before doing the final preparation for planting.

Planting

General planting can still be done in early winter, if not finished in late autumn but never when the ground is frozen or waterlogged.

Pruning ornamentals

If the large-flowered and cluster-flowered roses have grown rather leggy, it does no harm to shorten them back a few centimetres (inches) to prevent wind-rocking.

Shrub roses can also have done what little pruning may be needed, to tidy their outlines. Remove old growth and

Callicarpa bodinieri giraldii *has spectacular berries, but, sadly, they are seldom seen except in hot summers. The foliage has warm autumn tints.*

Above: *Make pruning cuts cleanly, as close as possible to a bud. Begin them on the side opposite to the bud.*
Below: *An amber-yellow-berried form of the guelder rose,* Viburnum opulus *Fructu luteo fruits in autumn.*

any shoots which are badly diseased or cluttering up the bush, preventing the good new growth from getting the light and air available.

Wisteria which was partially pruned in summer can be finished now by cutting back the shortened shoots to leave 5 or 7.5cm (2 or 3in) of stem. This method of pruning gradually builds up a spur system, and in time a few of the oldest spurs should be cut right away, once they begin to flower badly.

Climbing honeysuckle can be thinned now by cutting one or two of the oldest stems right out, and removing dead, diseased and weak shoots.

Campsis is mostly spur-pruned, with the new shoots cut back to stumps like wisteria, once the main shoots have filled the space allowed, but about four or five strong new shoots are left full length to clothe the support, and plant.

Summer-flowering jasmine can be treated now, if missed earlier (see Mid-Autumn), but in cold districts it is better to leave it until spring.

Pruning fruit

Once the leaves have fallen and the trees have become dormant, pruning can safely be done, even in frosty weather, provided it is not severely cold.

Trees which were framework-grafted in the spring should be pruned by cutting the new growth from the grafted shoots at the ends of the main branches by a quarter to one third its length; one third of the remaining new shoots, spaced evenly over the tree, should be cut to about half their length, and any further sucker growth or badly placed grafts should be completely removed. In future winters, renewal prune in the usual way, as for bush apples and pears.

Apples and pears

Apples and pears, cordon- and espalier-trained. The new shoots partially cut back in summer can now be shortened to about 7.5-10cm (3-4in) if they are primary side-shoots, but if secondary, should be reduced to about 2cm (1in). The leading shoots should be kept cut back, if need be, to the space available.

Apples and pears, bush trees. The most productive method for the amount of labour involved is the system of pruning called renewal, based on the fact that a shoot will fruit in its third year. The object of this pruning is to get a good supply of new side-shoots growing all the time to replace, or renew, the fruiting wood.

At the end of the summer a new shoot will have leaves all along it. During the following summer—the second one—buds will grow in the axils of these leaves; they will be round and fat, and are blossom buds. At the same time the tip bud will grow out to produce a new length of stem. In the third summer, the blossom buds will flower and fruit, growing out as they do so on a short length of stem, the beginning of a spur. The second summer's new growth, at the tip of the shoot, will form blossom buds, and at the same time, its own extension of the stem at the tip.

By cutting back the two-year-old growth and three-year-old growth, the amount of fruit produced can be manipulated and the production of vegetative growth regulated, so that there is a balance in the tree each season between fruit and shoot production. Heavy cutting encourages shoots to form and takes away potential fruit; very light pruning can result in overcropping and no renewal of shoots.

Depending on the vigour of the tree, about one-third to a half of the two- and three-year-old shoots can be cut, to leave about four or five fruit buds on the two-year-old growth, and one fruit bud or spur on the older. The growth at the ends of the main branches, the leaders, is pruned by one-third, a half, or two-thirds, depending on whether it is strong, moderate or weak, until its full length is reached. Then it is treated like a side-shoot.

The weather, the soil, the feeding programme, the rootstock and the variety will all affect the fruiting potential of the tree; if you find that the amount of pruning you are doing each winter is producing too much fruit or too much leaf, it must be adjusted, remembering that the more pruning, on the whole, the less fruit and the more shoots.

Apricots, fan-trained. Most of the pruning for these is done in spring and summer, but after fruiting or in early winter, one or two of the oldest main branches can be taken away completely, not necessarily every year.

Morello cherry, fan-trained. Cut very long bare shoots, which have been fruiting badly, back hard to a conveniently placed dormant bud, untie the remaining shoots, and re-tie, evenly spaced. Cut out any of these which are crowded.

Figs, fan-trained. Little needs to be done to figs in winter. New growth is constantly required for fruiting, so two or three of the oldest branches forming some of the ribs of the fan can be cut right down to leave stubs with dormant buds on them. Any shoots with long bare sections which are unlikely to be covered by other new growth are cut to below the bare section, and new shoots should appear from the remaining stem.

Grape vines, wall grown. Once the leaves have fallen, vines can be pruned by cutting the side-shoots back to a stump with one or two buds on it, and the topmost leading shoot back by about two thirds.

Liriodendron tulipifera (*tulip tree*) *is a hardy deciduous tree from North America, up to 60m (200ft) tall.*

Small Trees

Name	Height metres/ft	Time of flowering; flower colour	Fruit/foliage	Soil/aspect
Bay, sweet (*Laurus nobilis*)	5-9m (15-30ft)	Late spring; creamy	Evergreen; culinary	Any soil; sun and shelter
Cornelian cherry (*Cornus mas*)	5-6m (15-19ft)	Late winter—early spring; yellow	Variegated and yellow-leaved forms available	Any soil; and site
Cotoneaster (*Hybridus pendulus*)	3m (10ft)	Early—mid-summer; cream	Semi-evergreen; red berries	Any soil; shelter
Crabapple (Malus spp.)	5-7.5m (15-25ft)	Mid—late spring; white, pink, red	Green or purple; good fruit, edible	Any soil and site
Eucryphia	3.5-9m (12-30ft)	Late summer; white	Evergreen	Acid soil; sun or some shade; shelter from wind
Hawthorn (May) Crataegus spp.)	3.5-7.5m (12-25ft)	Late spring—early summer; white, pink, red, some double	Red berries	Any soil and site
Holly (Ilex spp.)	3-7.5m (15-25ft) (slow-growing)	Flowers inconspicuous	Evergreen; some variegated, red berries	Any soil; sun or some shade
Judas tree (*Cercis siliquastrum*)	6m (19ft)	Late spring; purple-pink	Flat, dark-red seed pods in autumn	Any soil; sun
Laburnum in variety	5-7.5m (15-25ft)	Late spring—early summer; yellow, some fragrant	Seeds poisonous	Well-drained soil; sun
Magnolia in variety	3-6.5m (10-20ft)	Early spring—early autumn; white, purple, pink; some fragrant	Some evergreen	Preferably acid soil; sun; shelter from wind
Maple, Japanese (*Acer palmatum* in variety)	1.5-2m (4-7ft) (slow-growing)	Flowers inconspicuous	Ornamental leaves	Preferably acid soil; shelter from wind; any aspect
Mountain ash (*Sorbus aucuparia* in variety)	5-9m (15-30ft)	Late spring—early summer; cream	Red, yellow, pink berries	Any aspect and soil
Parrotia persica	5m (15ft) spreading	Late winter—early spring; red but insignificant	Good autumn leaf colour	Any soil and site
Pear, ornamental (*Pyrus salicifolia pendula*)	7.5-9m (25-30ft) weeping, slow		Silver-grey leaves	Well-drained soil; any site
Prunus in variety (almond, cherry, plum)	3-7.5m (10-25ft)	Early—late spring; white, pink, yellow, red	Leaves green, red, purple	Any soil and site
Strawberry tree (*Arbutus unedo*)	5m (15ft)	Mid-autumn—early winter; white, fruit at the same time as the flowers	Evergreen; red fruit	Any soil and site
Whitebeam (*Sorbus aria*)	5-6m (15-19ft)	White; spring	Silver-grey leaves	Any soil and site
Willow (*Salix purpurea pendula*)	5-6m (15-19ft)	Flowers inconspicuous	Blue-green	Any moist soil

Medlar, mulberry and quince. Virtually no pruning is needed for these fruits, beyond the standard treatment of clearing out weak, crowded, dead, diseased or crossing growth. All will fruit satisfactorily without further cutting.

Peaches and nectarines, fan-trained. These can be pruned immediately after picking the fruit, or after leaf-fall. The shoots which have fruited are cut back to the replacement shoot and each of these spaced out regularly and tied to the wires. If crowding is unavoidable, some thinning of these shoots can be done.

Saving scions

If you are proposing to framework-graft apples or pears in the spring to change the variety, the one-year-old shoots cut off in the course of renewal pruning can be used as scions. They should be strong and mature. Heel them in, tied in small bundles, about 15cm (6in) deep in a trench on the north side of a fence or wall; label them securely.

Protecting

From now until spring, it will be necessary to keep an eye on supports and protection of tender plants, climbers and those which are favoured by birds. Plants vulnerable to

Protecting plants: a sheet of glass for small alpine plants, sacking right round larger plants, or two rolls of wire netting, padded with straw or bracken and staked.

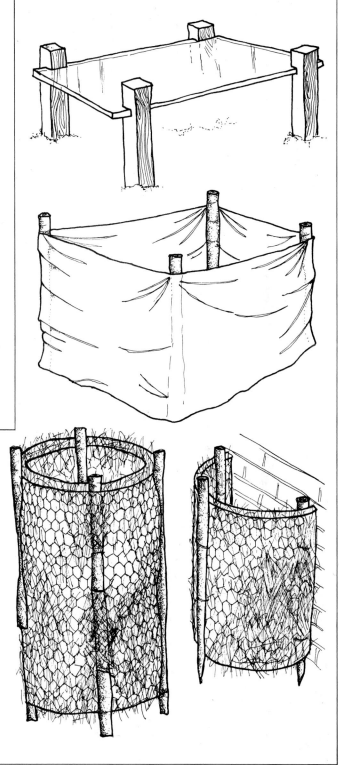

cold, especially north and east winds, are: *Abelia grandiflora*, campsis, ceanothus, *Clematis armandii*, eccremocarpus, escallonia, fremontodendron, fuchsia, hebe (some), hibiscus, summer jasmine, Mexican orange blossom (choisya), phlomis, piptanthus, privet, rock rose (cistus), romneya, *Senecio greyi*, solanum and yucca. All these need some sort of protection.

Weather damage can be in the form of rocking, when hollows form round the trunk or stem bases, which fill up with water and rot the bark, or plants being lifted by frost after planting. Snow and wind can break shoots and branches; bark can split due to cold (cover wound with sealing compound or glasshouse sealing tape), and young shoots are burned by strong cold wind.

Protection against birds may be destroyed by the weather, so renew sprays after heavy rain or snow and make sure that netting is still tightly secured and without unwanted holes after wind.

A double-flowered form of the almond, Prunus triloba, *needs to be pruned hard after flowering to encourage the production of new flowering shoots.* P. triloba *is one of a genus of about 430 species of trees and shrubs, including almonds, apricots, cherries, peaches, plums and nectarines, and ornamental plants such as cherry-laurel.*

Sweeping up
Leaves may still be in need of sweeping up, after a late fall, or burning, if diseased.

Increasing
When pruning vines, cuttings can be made and used now or stored for increase later. Mature one-year-old shoots are used, to provide cuttings about 30cm (12in) long; these are put in to half their length in a sheltered place outdoors or in a cold frame. In good conditions, these will root without any further ado, but if not, they can be used to provide vine 'eyes' in late winter.

Treating pests and diseases
Once the pruning is finished, tree and climbing fruits can be winter washed if necessary (see spray chart in Mid-Winter).

To prevent rose black spot and rust overwintering, as far as possible, leaves, fallen shoots and flowers should be raked up from round the plants and burnt. If the large-flowered and cluster-flowered roses are fully dormant, they can be sprayed with a solution of Bordeaux mixture, but it should not be applied if there are still leaves on the plants.

Vines should be brushed down thoroughly with a stiff brush before spraying or painting to get rid of loose bark in which pests and diseases can lurk.

Plants in flower
Cherry (autumn-flowering, *Prunus subhirtella autumnalis*), Fatsia, Heather (*Calluna vulgaris*, *Erica carnea* varieties), Jasmine (winter-flowering, *Jasminum nudiflorum*), Laurustinus, Mahonia Charity, Roses, *Viburnum farreri* and *V. Dawn*, Winter sweet (*Chimonanthus praecox*), Witch hazel (*Hamamelis mollis*)

Fruits in store
Apple, Medlar, Pear, Quince

Mid-Winter

Mid-winter is not a good time for outdoor gardening; if the ground is not covered in snow, it is likely to be frozen hard or so wet that it is waterlogged. There are often strong and penetratingly cold winds blowing or thick mist or fog, making it thoroughly unpleasant to be out-of-doors. However, the occasional, sunny, less cold day does occur and mid-winter can be unnaturally mild, resulting in cold and snow in early and mid-spring.

When the weather does improve, you can take the opportunity to finish pruning, do some basic digging and even plant, if the soil is workable; otherwise heel the plants in.

Weather damage should be checked and plant protection, supports and ties reinforced or repaired. Fruit in store should not be forgotten, neither should stratified seeds.

Once pruning is finished, tree fruit can have a winter wash applied to it, if thought necessary. However, unless moss and lichen on the bark of the trees has become very thick, it is preferable to rely on a lightning attack with a spray during the growing season, and let the beneficial insects do most of the work for you.

At~a~glance diary

Prepare the soil for:	planting by double digging, manuring at the same time and liming if necessary (but do not lime at the same time as adding manure)
Plant:	hardy deciduous plants if the weather permits, such as deciduous shrubs and ornamental trees, climbers, roses, hedging plants and fruit trees
Prune ornamentals:	cut back climbing ornamentals, such as overgrown or crowded honeysuckle, finish pruning of wisteria begun in summer, and prune campsis and summer jasmine before really cold weather;
Prune fruit:	apple, Morello cherry, medlar, mulberry, pear and quince; finish pruning as early in this season as possible apricot, fig, nectarine, peach and vine
Protect:	plants against birds, cold, wind, bark gnawing by small/large mammals
Pests and diseases:	black spot and rust on roses; spray apples, pears, cherries, plums, greengages and other tree fruits with tar-oil winter wash to control over-wintering eggs of aphids and apple sucker and adult scale insects; spray vines with sulphur to control scale insects, and with soft soap for mealy bug
Check:	stored fruit for damage; stratified seed for attack by mice
Plan:	garden design and/or cropping programme

Jobs to do

Preparing the ground for planting

Basic digging can be started or continued (see Early Winter for method). If the addition of lime will be necessary, digging should be finished as soon as possible, to allow for several weeks between adding organic material and lime.

Planting

If the weather allows, you can plant any of the woody plants except the evergreens; once planted they must have protection from wind and some protection from frost would be advisable, though snow will act as a protective blanket. If plants have arrived just as the weather becomes unsuitable, heel them in for the time being (see Planting, Late autumn).

Pruning

By now the pruning of the tree fruits and climbing ornamentals should be finished or well on the way to it. Grape vines in particular should be finished as soon as possible.

Training

Grape vines which were pruned in early winter should now be partially untied from their supports and allowed to hang downwards for about half their length. This is to make certain that when the buds begin to sprout, growth occurs evenly the whole length of the stem (rod), otherwise too many strong shoots are produced near its end and very few lower down. However, tie them in loosely to prevent wind damage.

Protecting

It is even more important now than in early winter to make sure that plants are safeguarded against bud pecking

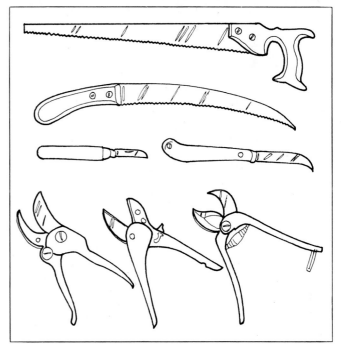

Above, right: Ivy climbs until it reaches the light and then become tree-like, when it flowers in late summer. Right: Tools for pruning include rolcut or parrot-billed secateurs, knives, and various types of saw, including both the folding saw and the rigid straight saw.

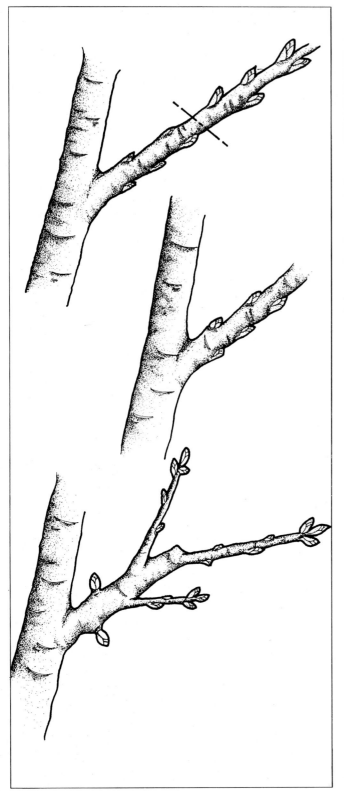

Above: *Berries of* Viburnum davidii *last through winter.*
Left: *Results of pruning. A shoot left unpruned fruits in the third year of its life all along the portion which grew in the first year. If cut, it produces some fruit buds (round and fat) and some new shoots from this length of stem.*
Opposite: *This lawn is shaded by the branches of an apple tree, with euphorbias and ferns clustered at its foot.*

by birds, that supports and ties are secure and strong and that the tender plants have sufficient coverings to enable them to shrug off frost and cold wind.

If real cold has set in, trouble with bark gnawing will start as the small mammals, such as rabbits, hares, mice, voles and rats, begin to run out of their normal food. Young plants recently put in are particularly vulnerable, with their narrow trunks or main stems, from which the bark is easily eaten or torn off in a complete circle. A mature plant will have some difficulty in recovering from this kind of onslaught, but a young one will more than likely be dead by the end of winter.

A cylinder of wire-netting of 1.2cm ($\frac{1}{2}$in) mesh put round the trunk and reaching up to the head, even of a standard, will stop most of the damage. Bush trees sometimes have their lowest branches attached by hares, which are quite capable of standing on their hind legs and leaning on the wire-netting while they gnaw, but this is less serious than attack on the main trunk.

Control Guide to Fruit Troubles

Time to spray	Troubles	Treatment
APPLES AND PEARS		
early—late winter (dormant)	aphids, scale and apple sucker	5% tar-oil winter wash
early spring—mid-spring (bud burst to green cluster stage of apple or early white bud stage of pear)	caterpillar (including winter and March moths)	derris
	aphids, apple sucker, capsid bugs, scale insects and pear midge;	derris or bioresmethrin
	mildew	benomyl or dinocap
repeat every 2 weeks until mid-summer	scab disease	benomyl or captan
mid-spring—start of late spring (pink bud stage of apple, petal fall stage of pear)	mildew	benomyl or dinocap
mid-spring—late spring (80% petal fall stage of apple)	apple sawfly	derris
	mildew	benomyl or dinocap
start of early summer	red spider mite	derris
	mildew	benomyl or dinocap
	codling moth	derris
2-3 weeks later (mid-summer)	red spider mite — repeat	derris
	codling moth	sacking bands round tree trunks
early autumn	winter and March moths	greasebands
PLUMS AND DAMSONS		
early—late winter (dormant)	aphids	5% tar-oil winter wash
early spring (bud burst to white bud stage)	caterpillars	derris
	aphids	derris or bioresmethrin
late spring (cotyledon split)	sawfly	derris
late spring (post blossom)	red spider mite	derris
10 days later	red spider mite — repeat	derris
early summer	red plum maggot	derris
2 weeks later	red plum maggot — repeat	derris
CHERRIES		
early—late winter	aphids	5% tar-oil winter wash
mid-spring—late spring	caterpillars	derris
(bud burst to white bud stage)	aphids	derris or bioresmethrin
late summer and twice more at 3-week intervals	bacterial canker	Bordeaux mixture
PEACHES, NECTARINES AND APRICOTS		
early—late winter (dormant)	aphids	5% tar-oil winter wash
mid-winter (bud swelling stage)	peach leaf-curl disease	Bordeaux mixture or lime sulphur
2 weeks later	peach leaf-curl disease — repeat	Bordeaux mixture or lime sulphur
early—mid-spring	caterpillars, aphids	derris or bioresmethrin
mid-spring (petal fall stage)	red spider mite	derris
early summer	aphids	bioresmethrin or quassia
mid-summer	aphids	bioresmethrin or quassia
early autumn (just before leaf fall)	peach leaf-curl disease	Bordeaux mixture or lime sulphur
GRAPE VINE		
early winter	scale	sulphur
	mealy bug	soft soap
early spring	mildew	dinocap, benomyl or sulphur
mid-spring	mildew — repeat	dinocap, benomyl or sulphur
late spring	mildew — repeat	dinocap, benomyl
early summer	red spider mite	derris
	mildew	dinocap, benomyl
3 weeks later and at similar intervals as	red spider mite — repeat	derris
necessary until the end of summer	mildew	dinocap, benomyl
throughout growing season	vine weevil	carbaryl
whenever present		
as above	mealy bug	methylated spirits

Cylinders made of plastic, with ventilation holes in them, can be obtained and used instead of netting. They may be more effective in preventing damage by mice, but it is advisable to lift the cylinders occasionally and make sure the mice have not adopted them as a highly convenient nesting place, with food ready to hand.

There are harmless repellents for small mammals, applied in liquid or powder form, and if you live in an area where deer roam wild, these repellents can be used against them also. Deer can be a great problem to shrubs and trees and sometimes the only solution is a 1.8m (6ft) high barrier all round the orchard or entire garden.

Corylopsis spicata prefers an acid or neutral soil, but will grow in a chalky one, provided it is deep.

Treating pests and diseases

Once fruit trees become fully dormant, they can be sprayed with a winter wash of tar-oil, if thought necessary. However, it has been found that such a wash kills the over-wintering forms of a good many beneficial insects which are predators of the pests and it also destroys the mosses and lichen on which red spider mite feeds in summer. Thus, with the removal of predators and its natural food, the mite attacks leaves and builds up very large populations in summer. This seriously weakens the trees but, unfortunately, chemical control is now very difficult as the mite is resistant to the sprays based on phosphorus, such as malathion and dimethoate.

Tar-oil washes now are mainly used for removing lichens and moss from mature and old trees and should only be used occasionally.

The control programme which follows gives details of various troubles which may occur on tree fruits and grape vines, the control method and the time to apply it. However, there is no need to use all the chemicals mentioned every year; in fact, it is preferable not to. Apply them only as a preventive, if trouble occurred the year before, in the case of scab, mildew, peach-leaf curl and bacterial canker. For insect pests, such as greenfly and caterpillars, it is generally sufficient to spray or treat when the first one or two are seen, but for sawfly, codling moth, red spider mite, red plum maggot and capsid, they should automatically be applied when suggested.

It is quite possible to obtain perfectly adequate fruit crops without doing any spraying at all, particularly if you ensure that the trees are properly pruned, fed and watered all through their lives. They may not be completely free of the odd spot or nibble but a natural balance will be set up between beneficial and damaging insects, so that no one species gets out of hand. The fungus diseases can cause more trouble, but even so, a constitutionally strong tree will be much less badly infected.

Checking

Some varieties of apples and pears may have been in store now for three months and a thorough looking-over will decrease wastage from rots, frost and attack by mice and rats. Seeds which have been stratified will not be harmed by cold; the colder it is the better, as this 'vernalization', as it is called, is nature's way of breaking dormancy. Without it some seeds never germinate. However, hungry mice can quietly decimate your seed collection, and a check to make sure the frame gauze or netting is in place takes only a minute or two.

Planning

You can take the opportunity resulting from this lull in active gardening to do some thinking and planning, to look back over your garden notebook for the year and consider changes or innovations in the garden layout or cropping plan. One of the fascinations of gardening is that you can always improve on your garden's appearance, as your experience and knowledge increases.

Specialist books, catalogues from specialist nurseries, the year books of specialist societies such as those for roses, camellias, fruit, and so on, will all supply more information and more help for good cultivation. New methods of growing some plant or other frequently appear, new ways and chemicals for controlling or preventing disease and pest trouble are regularly produced and new hybrids and varieties provide mouth-watering choices every year.

Cercidiphyllum japonicum *is an easily-grown tree,* $4\frac{1}{2}$*-12m (15-40ft) high, with good autumn leaf colouring.*

Plants in flower

Cherry (autumn-flowering, Prunus subhirtella autumnalis), Garrya elliptica, Heather (Erica carnea in variety), Jasmine (winter-flowering, Jasminum nudiflorum), Laurustinus, Viburnum farreri and V. Dawn, Winter sweet (Chimonanthus praecox), witch hazel (Hamamelis mollis)

Fruits in store

Apple, Pear, Quince

Late Winter

After the peace of mid-winter, there begins to be a definite feeling of revival in the air in late winter. Even if there is still snow about, the days are appreciably longer and the earliest shrub and tree buds, willow, clematis and perhaps even roses, will begin to sprout towards the end of this season. You will need to finish the winter pruning as near the beginning of late winter as possible and some advance rose pruning may be necessary.

Similarly, planting of deciduous shrubs and trees should be finished, digging completed, and winter tar-oil spraying must be got out of the way before the buds begin to unfold, otherwise they will be damaged.

With the rising of the sap, there are two new jobs to do which would not have been of much benefit done earlier: feeding the tree fruit and mulching some of the shrubs and climbers. Vacant soil can also be treated, with lime.

At~a~glance diary

Prepare the soil for: planting heeled-in plants now, or for planting in early spring such subjects as the hardier evergreens and deciduous shrubs and trees; also double dig if not already done for planting tender shrubs in mid-spring–late spring

Plant: deciduous shrubs, trees and climbers, provided that the ground is not water-logged, frozen or covered in snow

Prune: finish tree fruits; finish climbing ornamentals as for Early Winter; also prune Abelia x grandiflora, clematis, Garrya elliptica, japonica, winter jasmine, roses (early seasons)

Feed: tree fruit, vines, with a compound or straight fertilizer as necessary

Lime: acidic soils

Check: protection against birds, cold, wind, mammals; check ties and supports

Increase: vines from vine 'eyes'

Pests and diseases: spray tar-oil winter wash on fruit trees (not apricots, nectarines or peaches) as early as possible, as it will damage shoots and leaves which may soon appear; spray apricots, peaches and nectarines with fungicide for peach leaf curl; spray vines against scale or mealy bug if not already done

Jobs to do

Preparing the ground for planting

As you may still have heeled-in plants to put in or may be expecting new arrivals in early spring, such as evergreens, the ground will need forking and dressing with bonemeal (see Mid-Autumn). If it is still hard with frost, covered with snow or sodden, wait until soil conditions improve.

It is rather late to do basic digging, unless it is of ground in which you intend to plant tender shrubs in mid- or late spring; the two- to three-month gap in that case will be sufficient to allow the soil to digest the organic matter and other nutrients added and settle down again.

Planting

Although late autumn and, to some extent, early winter, are the best times for planting, deciduous woody plants (unless tender) can be put in at any time when dormant. The only restrictions are the state of the soil and very bad weather. If you do plant now, make sure those that need it are firmly supported and protected against prevailing winds which, with the change of season in a few weeks' time, will begin to blow with gale force strength.

Pruning

If tree fruit pruning is not finished in late winter, it will be too late to do it afterwards without damaging the trees and upsetting their management. Wisteria should be pruned, if not yet done, together with other climbing ornamentals mentioned in Early Winter. Other shrubs to prune now include the following:

Abelia x *grandiflora* At the end of late winter, these can be tidied up by cutting off weak new shoots completely, cutting back long shoots and removing one or two of the oldest stems to ground level in some years. In cold seasons and districts, wait until late in early spring before doing this.

Clematis The large-flowered kinds which flower from late in early summer right through almost until autumn will probably start to sprout this season, if they have not already done so; some shoots, in early seasons, can be

The camellia's flowers may be pink, white, red, rose-pink or striped with any of these colours. It grows in acid or neutral soil, with a little shade and protection from the sun in the early morning in spring.

30cm (12in) long by now. Even if they are, the main stems should still be cut hard back to within 90cm (36in) of the ground, to just above a pair of buds. As they are very low down on the stems, this pair of buds will probably be still dormant, but cutting will encourage sprouting.

The large-flowered clematis that flower in late spring and early summer do better with much less ruthless treatment. Since it will now be possible to see where the dead growth is, this can be cut off; the live new shoots are then cut back to remove not much more than the tips, to just above the first pair of dormant buds. To make the most of their flowering display, these shoots should then be spread out evenly and separately and tied in position.

Clematis planted in autumn and earlier in the winter should now be cut back hard to just above a pair of still dormant buds, about 15–30cm (6–12in) above ground.

Garrya elliptica Pruning of this is mainly to prevent the bush becoming too crowded, as it is enthusiastic about growing, so some catkin-bearing growth should be removed as soon as the catkins have finished, to let in light and air, and some of the oldest shoots can be completely removed. Pruning should always be done before new growth begins.

Japonica The tendency of this shrub to produce thin, straggly shoots without flowers needs checking, so such growth can be cut back now before flowering, to leave a stub with one or two buds on it. Watch for the flower buds, which will be round and fat.

Above: *The evergreen hedging plants, such as box or yew, are very suitable for topiary work of the kind shown here.* Below: *Stretch a line taut along the top of a hedge as a guide for keeping the top level while you trim it.*

Winter jasmine As soon as this has finished flowering, which may not be until early spring, cut the strong flowered shoots back by about three-quarters of their length and the remainder to leave stubs with one or two pairs of buds on them. Alternatively, this rather hard pruning can be replaced by simply thinning some of the flowered shoots, to give the remainder room to breathe. In this case when pruning, remove about half the length of flowered shoot.

Roses In some seasons and some districts, pruning of large-flowered and cluster-flowered kinds can start during late winter. Climbers can have what little pruning they need done at the same time; dead growth is cut off, flowering growth which has become too old to flower well should be cut back to a strong new shoot, and small side-shoots can be cut to about 7.5cm (3in) or one bud.

Feeding

Late winter is an appropriate time to feed tree fruits, if they need it. If the soil was carefully prepared before planting and is subsequently regularly topdressed with rotted organic matter fertilizers may not be necessary at all. However, sandy or shallow soils are likely to need annual additions of fertilizer, unless you are clever with the use of manure or garden compost.

The leaves of the stag's-horn sumach, Rhus typhina, *turn to glorious shades of orange and then crimson in autumn. The fruiting spikes also turn crimson.*

Main mineral nutrients needed are nitrogen, phosphorus and potassium and these can be obtained singly as, for example, sulphate of ammonia (nitrogen, N) or sulphate of potash (potassium, K), or as compounds containing all three in varying percentages. The percentage will be shown on the container in the form of an 'analysis'—thus: N 5 per cent, P_2O_5 (phosphorus, P) 7 per cent, K_2O 9 per cent, so helping you to decide which is the most suitable for your plants.

Nitrogen helps with shoot and leaf growth, phosphorus is needed by the roots and potassium is the maturing nutrient, encouraging flower and fruit production. These divisions are very general and the subject of nutrients and their interaction is extremely complex, but remembering that the above are the main roles of these nutrients, you can apply them according to whether your plants are cropping too much, moderately, or running to leaf.

Rates of application of the compound fertilizers will be given on their containers; the 'straights' are applied as follows:

Sulphate of ammonia (N),
     15–30g per sq m ($\frac{1}{2}$–1oz per sq yd)
Nitro-chalk (N and lime) 30g per sq m (1oz per sq yd)
Hoof-and-horn meal (N) 60g per sq m (2 oz per sq yd)
Superphosphate (P) 30–90g per sq m (1–3oz per sq yd)
Bonemeal (P)   up to 180g per sq m (6oz per sq yd)
Sulphate of potash (K) 15–30g per sq m ($\frac{1}{2}$–1oz per sq yd)
Wood ash (K)   up to 240g per sq m (8oz per sq yd)

Nitro-chalk is a convenient way of ensuring that the stone fruits get the calcium they need but if nitro-chalk is not used, lime should be applied every four or five years or so at about 240g per sq m (8oz per sq yd), depending on the degree of acidity of the soil.

There are many other mineral nutrients also required by plants; some are called the 'trace' elements as the plant requires them only in minute quantities, to the order of parts per million, and others such as sulphur, iron and calcium are the minor elements, coming between the two. All have different functions within the plants and are dependent on one another to some extent and all are present in the average garden soil, provided it is treated with rotted organic matter in sufficient quantity to ward off deficiencies.

If the state of the soil permits, grape vines can also be fed and topdressed. Weeds, leaves, last spring's mulch remains and other rubbish should be raked carefully off the area beneath which the roots are growing. Then a mixture of rotted organic matter and loam in equal parts, combined with a proprietary vine compound fertilizer, can be spread over the clean soil surface to a depth of about 7.5cm (3in).

Liming

Soil that is proved by a soil test to be very acid in its reaction can be treated by liming so that it becomes only slightly acid. This degree of acidity is probably the most suitable one for growing the widest range of woody plants; tree fruits, the ericaceous plants such as rhododendrons and most of the heathers, in particular, do not do well on

Left: Winter flowers are often fragrant, and the winter sweet, Chimonanthus praecox, *is no exception.* Opposite: *The Kurume azaleas are a selection of some of the best and grow superbly in light woodland conditions.*

Layering a clematis: Use a shoot at least 18 months old, bend it to form a U, peg it down into a potful of compost, and plunge the pot. Do not layer in cold weather.

chalky soils or those with a markedly alkaline reaction. If you have a choice, choose a neutral to mildly acidic soil when planting.

Be very careful not to overlime, as reduction of alkalinity is a slow and difficult process; from the soil-testing kit you will know the quantity to apply, depending on the degree of acidity. Ground limestone or chalk are slow acting and can be used at up to 1 kg per square m (2 lb per sq yd), though this amount is a rather heavy dressing.

Do not apply lime until at least six weeks have elapsed since the application of organic matter and do not apply at the same time as sulphate of ammonia, basic slag or super-phosphate.

Checking

Routine checks of protections of various kinds, supports and ties are advisable some time in late winter. Bark gnawing may still be a serious potential problem, as the animals get hungrier towards the end of winter.

Increasing

The only plant which can be multiplied now is the grape vine and then only if you can supply warmth. The hard-

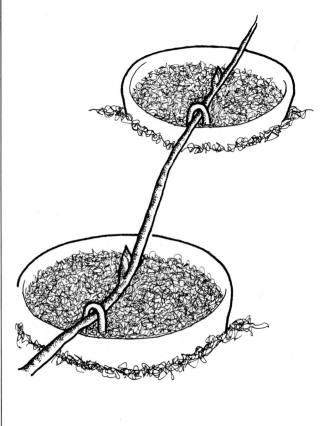

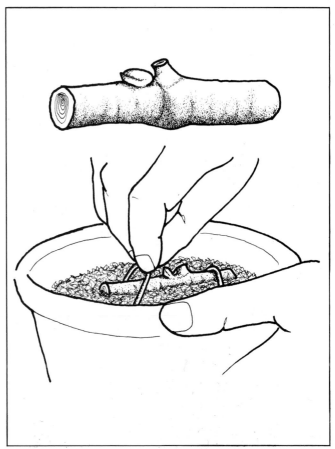

Above, left: Cornelian cherry, Cornus mas, is a small tree which flowers in late winter, and has bright red, edible fruits in hot summers. In autumn, the leaves are a red-purple. Above, right: Vines can be increased from vine 'eyes'. Cut a short length of stem with a dormant bud, pin it down in compost, and it will root with the help of heat.

wood cuttings made in early winter can be used to supply 5cm (2in) lengths of shoot, each with a bud or 'eye' on it. The cutting is pegged down into cuttings compost in a 7.5cm (3in) pot. In a temperature of 10–15°C (50–60°F) and with bottom heat of 21°C (70°F) supplied to the compost rooting will take about three weeks.

Treating pests and diseases

If you propose to use a tar-oil winter wash on fruit trees in winter, to cut out some of the summer spraying and to clean the trees of mosses and lichens, it should be applied early this season, as it damages leaves and young shoots which can soon start to appear. Peaches, nectarines and apricots may need a fungicidal spray against leaf-curl, put on just before the buds sprout and repeated two weeks later to cover the young developing leaves (see chart in Mid-Winter for control of fruit troubles and treatment section at end of book).

Plants in flower

Camellia (shelter), Cornelian cherry (Cornus mas), Cherry (Autumn-flowering, Prunus subhirtella autumnalis), Clematis, Honeysuckle (Lonicera standishii), Japonica (Chaenomeles speciosa), Jasmine (winter-flowering, Jasminum nudiflorum), Laurustinus, Mahonia japonica (shelter), Rhododendron, Sarcococca, Skimmia (shelter), Viburnum farreri, V. Dawn, Winter sweet (Chimonanthus praecox), Witch hazel (Hamamelis mollis)

Fruits in store

Apple, Pear, Quince

A Small Selection of Flowering & Foliage Shrubs

Name	Height spread cm/in	Time of flowering; flower colour	Foliage/bark/ berries	Soil/aspect	Remarks
Azalea in variety	45-150 x 45-120cm (18-60 x 18-48in)	mid-spring—early summer; all colours except blue	some evergreen	acid soil; light shade	
Berberis	30-300 x 30-300cm (12-120 x 12-120cm)	spring, summer; orange, yellow	some evergreen, leaves coloured; berries red or blue	any soil and aspect	
Broom (Cytisus and Genista spp.)	prostrate 270 x 60-300cm (108 x 24-120in)	spring—summer; yellow, pink, white	some have bright green stems	well-drained soil; sun	not very limy soil
Buddleia in variety	180-240 x 150cm (72-96 x 60in)	early—late summer; purple, blue, red, white, orange		any soil and aspect	*B. globosa* needs shelter
Camellia in variety	300 x 180cm (120 x 72in)	early—mid-spring; pink, white, red	evergreen	acid/neutral soil; light shade	shelter from north and east
Ceanothus in variety	120-360 x 150-210cm (58-144 x 60-84in)	mid-spring—autumn; blue	some evergreen	well-drained soil; sun	some slightly tender
Cistus in variety (rock rose)	90-240 x 90-150cm (36-96 x 36-60in)	late spring—mid-summer; pink, white, purple	evergreen, aromatic	well-drained soil; sun	slightly tender
Clematis	From 300cm (120in) to 7.5m (8yd); some climbing	spring—summer; purple, blue, white, pink, red		any except light	some are better colour with north aspect
Deutzia in variety	90-180 x 90-150cm (36-72 x 36-60in)	late spring—early summer; white, pink, purple-pink		any soil and site	
Fuchsia in variety	30-300 x 30-240cm (12-120 x 12-96in)	mid-summer—early autumn; purple, red, white, pink magenta, blue-purple		any soil and aspect	slightly tender
Heather	From 12.5 x 45cm (5 x 18in) to 300 x 240cm (120 x 96in)	winter—mid-autumn; pink, red, purple, white	foliage yellow, red, orange, bronze, grey, green	acid soil; sun	add peat to soil
Hebe in variety	22.5-150 x 22.5-120cm (9-60 x 9-48in)	late spring, summer—autumn; purple, blue, white, pink, red, magenta	evergreen, green, grey yellow-variegated	any well-drained soil; sun	
Honeysuckle	300-600cm (120-240in) climbing; 90-300 x 90-240cm (36-120 x 36-96in) shrubby	early summer—mid-autumn, winter; red-purple, cream, yellow, orange; some fragrant	some evergreen, or variegated	most soils; a little shade	
Hydrangea (round-headed)	90-180 x 90-180cm (36-72 x 36-72in)	mid-summer—early autumn; red, pink, blue, white, mauve		moist soil; a little shade	good by the sea; blue varieties in acid soil

A Small Selection of Flowering & Foliage Shrubs

Name	Height spread cm/in	Time of flowering; flower colour	Foliage/bark/berries	Soil/aspect	Remarks
Hypericum in variety	30-150 x 120cm (12-60 x 48in)	mid-summer—early autumn; yellow	some evergreen	any soil; sun or little shade	*H. calycinum* invasive
Ivy (hedera) in variety	climbing	flowers inconspicuous	evergreen, some variegated cream or yellow	any soil; a little shade	small-leaved varieties slow-growing
Japonica (chaenomeles)	90-240 x 120-300cm (36-96 x 48-120in)	early—late spring; pink, red, white		any soil and site	
Jasmine, winter (*J. nudiflorum*)	360 x 300cm (144 x 120in)	late autumn/late winter; yellow		any soil and site	good facing north
Jew's mallow (kerria)	240 x 180cm (96 x 72in)	mid—late spring; yellow		any soil and site	double form the best
Lavender	45-90 x 60-120cm (18-36 x 24-48in)	mid—late summer; lavender, white, blue; fragrant	evergrey	well-drained soil; sun	
Lilac in variety	90-450 x 150-360cm (36-180 x 60-144in)	spring—summer; white, red, lilac; fragrant		any soil; sun or some shade	
Magnolia in variety (shrubby)	210-360 x 150-300cm (84-144 x 60-120in)	spring—early autumn; white, purple; some fragrant	some evergreen	acid soil; sun	need shelter
Mahonia in variety	120-300 x 150-210cm (48-120 x 60-84in)	winter—spring; yellow; fragrant	evergreen	any soil and site	do better with shelter
Mexican orange blossom (*Choisya ternata*)	180 x 120cm (72 x 84in)	late spring, early autumn; white; fragrant	evergreen	well-drained soil; sun	not quite hardy
Philadelphus (mock orange)	90-450 x 90-300cm (36-180 x 36-120in)	early—mid-summer; white; fragrant		any soil and site	
Pyracantha in variety	180-360 x 210-300cm (72-144 x 84-120in)	early summer; white	evergreen; berries red, orange, yellow	any soil; sun or some shade	good as wall plants
Rhododendron in variety	23-600 x 23-300cm (9-240 x 9-120in) as shrubs	late winter—late summer; all colours	evergreen	acid soil; a little shade	
Senecio greyi	90-120 x 120cm (36-48 x 48in)	early—mid-summer; yellow	evergrey	any soil; sun	not hardy in severe winters
Spiraea in variety	45-210 x 45-150cm (18-84 x 18-60in)	spring, mid—late summer; white, pink, red		any soil; sun or some shade	
Virginia creeper (*Parthenocissus quinquefolia*)	21m (70ft) climbing	inconspicuous flowers	brilliant autumn leaf colour	any soil and aspect	
Weigela (diervilla)	90-150 x 50-150cm (36-60 x 36-60in)	late spring—early summer; pink, red, white, salmon	one variety, yellow-leaved	any soil and site	
Wisteria	30m (100ft) climbing	spring—early summer, late summer; purple, white		rich moist soil; sun	
Witch hazel (hamamelis)	210-300 x 150-240cm (84-120 x 60-96in)	winter, autumn; yellow or bronze-red		acid soil; sun or some shade	slow-growing

Fruit Varieties

The following list of fruit varieties gives a description of the fruit, the season of flowering, the season of ripening, the period of storage (if any) and the names of suitable pollinators. A few varieties are self-fertile, others must have pollinators, and a few others will only set fruit with certain varieties, or need two different pollinating varieties. Fig, medlar, mulberry and quince are not included in the list, delicious though they are, because, in each case, there is only one variety available.

C=Culinary   D=Dessert

Name		Description	Season of flowering	Ripe	Storage	Pollinators
APPLE						
Bramley's Seedling	C	green	late spring	mid-autumn	late-autumn—mid-spring	Cox's Orange, Grenadier, Tydeman's Early Worcester (T.E.W.)
Cox's Orange Pippin	D	yellow, flushed orange	late spring	early—mid-autumn	mid-autumn—mid-winter	Sunset, Fortune, Grenadier, T.E.W.
d'Arcy Spice	D	brown-green	late spring	late in mid-autumn	late autumn—mid-spring	Winston
Egremont Russet	D	yellow, with brown russet	early in late spring	mid-autumn	late autumn—early winter	Fortune, James Grieve, Sunset
Fortune	D	yellow-striped red	late spring	early—mid-autumn		Cox's, James Grieve, Sunset, T.E.W.
Grenadier	C	yellow-green	late spring	late summer—early autumn		Cox's, Fortune, James Grieve
James Grieve	D	heavily striped red	late spring	early autumn		Egremont Russet, Fortune, Grenadier
Sturmer Pippin	D	pale green, some russet	late spring	late in mid-autumn	late autumn—mid-spring	T.E.W., Grenadier, Cox's, Fortune
Sunset	D	dull yellow, flushed red	late spring	mid-autumn	late autumn—early winter	James Grieve, Egremont Russet
Tydeman's Early Worcester (T.E.W.)	D	green, striped red	late spring	late summer		Grenadier, Cox's, James Grieve, Fortune
Winston	D	flushed and striped red	late spring	late autumn	early winter—early spring	d'Arcy Spice, Cox's
APRICOT						
Farmingdale		yellow-orange, pink-flushed	early spring	early in late summer		self-fertile
Moorpark		brown-orange	early spring	late summer		self-fertile
CHERRY						
Bigarreau Napoleon		yellow, flushed red	mid-spring	late summer		Merton Glory
Early Rivers		black	mid-spring	early summer		Merton Favourite
Merton Bigarreau		black	mid-spring	mid-summer		Merton Glory, Merton Favourite, Morello
Morello (cooking)		red	mid-spring	late summer		self-fertile
DAMSON						
Farleigh Damson		blue-black	mid—late spring	middle or early autumn		Shropshire Damson

Fruit Varieties

Shropshire Prune		blue-black	mid—late spring	middle of early autumn		self-fertile
GRAPE						
Black Hamburgh		black	early summer	late summer—early autumn		self-fertile
Buckland Sweetwater		green to pale yellow	early summer	middle of late summer		self-fertile
Royal Muscadine		green to pale yellow	early summer	early autumn		self-fertile
GREENGAGE						
Cambridge Greengage		green	mid-spring	late summer		Victoria plum
Jefferson's Gage		yellow-green	mid-spring	early autumn		Reine Claude de Bavay
Reine Claude de Bavay		yellow-green	mid-spring	mid-autumn		self-fertile
NECTARINE						
Humboldt		orange with red flush	mid-spring	late summer		self-fertile
Lord Napier		green -yellow, crimson flush	early in mid-spring	late summer		self-fertile
PEACH						
Duke of York		crimson	early-mid-spring	late in mid-summer		self-fertile
Peregrine		red with yellow flesh	early-mid-spring	early in late summer		self-fertile
Rochester		yellow, red flush	early-mid-spring	middle of late summer		self-fertile
PEAR						
Beurré Hardy	D	russet with red flush	mid-spring	early autumn	mid-autumn	Conference, Fertility
Catillac	C	green	late in mid-spring	late autumn	late autumn/mid-winter	Fertility, Williams', Beurré Hardy
Conference	D	pale green	mid-spring	early in mid-autumn	late autumn	self-fertile
Doyenné du Comice	D	yellow, pale red flush	mid-spring	pick late in early autumn	mid-late autumn	Conference, Fertility, Josephine de Malines, Beurré Hardy
Fertility	D	orange-brown	late in mid-spring	early in mid-autumn		Conference, Vicar of Winkfield
Jargonelle	D	pale yellow	mid-spring	late summer		Beurré Hardy, Conference
Josephine de Malines	D	yellow with grey russet	mid-spring	late in mid-autumn	late autumn—early winter	Conference, Comice, Fertility, Williams'
Vicar of Winkfield	C	green to yellow	early in mid-spring	late in mid-autumn	early—mid-winter	Easter Beurré, Conference
Williams' Bon Chrétien	D	pale yellow	mid-spring	early autumn		Josephine de Malines, Fertility, Conference
Winter Nelis	D	green-yellow	late in mid-spring	late in mid-autumn	late autumn—mid-winter	Beurré Hardy, Josephine de Malines
PLUM						
Czar	C	reddish purple	mid-spring	mid-summer		self-fertile
Kirke's Blue	D	reddish blue	late in mid-spring	early autumn		Farleigh Damson, Marjorie's Seedling
Marjorie's Seedling	C & D	black	late in mid-spring	early—mid-autumn		self-fertile
River's Early	C	blue-purple	mid-spring	mid-summer		self-fertile
Victoria	C & D	red	mid-spring	late summer		self-fertile

Controls & Treatments

Prevention is better than cure—if you follow this principle when growing plants, you will save yourself time and expense. A good start with proper planting, followed by ensuring that food and water are supplied as needed, combined with careful pruning and safeguarding against extreme weather conditions, will result in strong plants able to withstand pest and disease infestation with little or no appreciable effect.

Occasionally you may have to resort to a specific method of control, in epidemic years especially; try to choose the most natural method first and use chemicals only as a last resort. If you have to use chemicals regularly, it is a sign that your plant management is poor or that you are trying to grow plants unsuited to the conditions of your garden.

Insect pests can be divided into two groups: the suckers and the biters. Aphids (greenfly, blackfly, mealy plum aphis, woolly aphis), leafhoppers, scale and mealy bug are some of the suckers, which live on the sap they withdraw from leaves, shoots and sometimes flowers. Derris, bioresmethrin and quassia are some of the safest chemicals to use against such pests.

The biters are mostly caterpillars, also slugs, maggots, wasps and such insects as the rose leaf-cutting bee, rose chafer beetles and vine weevils. Derris can be used for most of these also and is most efficient when at its freshest and

Above, left: *Aphids of various kinds cause a great deal of trouble by sucking the sap from leaves. These green fly are shown in their winged and unwinged forms.* Above, right: *The tawny mining bee, a solitary bee, makes holes in soil and helps to pollinate blossom.*

there is a good quantity of rotenone present. If slugs **appear**, methiocarb pellets will be an effective control, or use grit on the soil round soft, vulnerable shoots.

Some of the fungus diseases can be very serious: these include honey fungus, cherry bacterial canker and fireblight, and control is more difficult. Others are persistent, needing regular spraying for several months, although the new systemic fungicide, benomyl, has proved to be very useful for these. Many fungicides are protective rather than eradicant and so need to be applied repeatedly.

Bacterial diseases are hardly troublesome on woody plants; virus diseases occur mostly in the tree fruits in such forms as 'chat' fruits and rubbery wood. However, nurserymen take great care to use clean stocks and scions and much of the fruit available in Britain has been cleared under the EMLA testing programme, run jointly by East Malling and Long Ashton fruit research stations.

Nutrient deficiencies are mainly of iron or magnesium and appear on plants growing in strongly alkaline soils;

they can be put right with sequestered compounds of these nutrients and by reducing the alkalinity with peat, acidic fertilizers and sulphur. Such remedies are long-term ones and need skill in use; it is better to test the soil before planting, so that you can put in plants appropriate to the soil acidity.

Harmless repellents can be used to ward off such small mammals as mice, rabbits and voles and larger ones, too—deer in particular; quassia, extremely bitter, is a good one. Aluminium ammonium sulphate, anthraquinone and thiram are others.

Remember that there is a whole army of 'beneficial' insects, which are predatory on the pests, working for you; the less you spray, the more they will thrive and so maintain a balance between the various insect species. Once you begin to spray, especially the tree fruits, you run a great risk of ensuring that one pest breeds unchecked; in a monotype planting of—say—apples, it then spreads rapidly.

Remember also that bees and other pollinating insects are harmed by most chemical sprays, so never spray when the plants are in flower, except possibly when most of the blossom has set or fallen, and then do it late in the evening. When you have finished spraying, clean thoroughly all the sprayers and apparatus used and keep all chemicals out of the reach of pets and children at all times. Also, make sure the containers remain clearly labelled.

Another group of chemicals you may wish to use are those contained in weedkillers. Some are undoubtedly very useful and so far their application has not appeared to harm the soil. Simazine will keep the ground clear of weeds for twelve months; paraquat and diquat will kill seedling, annual and small weeds by disrupting the mechanism which produces chlorophyll, and dichlobenil will keep the ground round certain shrubs, roses, and trees free of all weeds, including perennials, for at least the growing season.

The latest weed killing chemical, glyphosate, combines some of the virtues of paraquat and dichlobenil, since it kills the plants through the top growth but is inactivated when it reaches the soil and will effectively control perennials as well as annuals and small weeds. Even the most persistent of weeds, such as bindweed, ground-elder, oxalis and horsetail, succumb to it. It has no effect on the soil flora and fauna.

The following is a list of pests and diseases specific to certain shrubs, trees, fruit and roses; details are given of appearance, damage, life-history and control. Do not assume that they will all automatically ravage your plants; one or more may do so, in some years, but some you may never have to contend with.

The cockchafer beetle can do much damage by eating flowers; its grubs feed on the roots of plants.

Roses

Black spot: fungus disease; fringed black spots o.6cm ($\frac{1}{4}$in) wide on leaves. May start from early spring and can defoliate bushes in bad attacks. Pick off, rake up and burn infected leaves; spray with benomyl or captan as makers direct.
Canker: fungus disease; bark on stems cracked and flaking off in patches, especially near to soil level. Worst in humid districts and badly drained soil. Pare off with knife to healthy wood or cut infected shoots off to healthy growth.. Improve soil drainage and increase supplies of phosphorus, calcium and/or magnesium.
Chafer beetle: insect; large brown or black flying beetles, which eat holes in flowers, flower buds and leaves, present in late spring and early summer. Control difficult; HCH (BHC) sometimes helps.

Mildew on roses infects the leaves and flower stems, as well as the shoot stems; it can badly stunt a plant.

Leaf-cutting bee: insect; adults similar to honey bees, remove semi-circular pieces from edge of leaf for making nests. Effect on plant is negligible and control is unnecessary.

Leaf-rolling sawfly: insect; maggots feed in rolled-up leaf margins and leaves wither. In bad attacks much defoliation occurs. Adult lays eggs on leaves in late spring and mid-summer. Spray HCH (BHC) at two- to three-week intervals to prevent adults laying eggs, otherwise hand-pick infested leaves as soon as seen and destroy.

Mildew: fungus disease; white powdery patches on young leaves and tips of shoots from early spring; flower buds and flowers can also be infected. Disease spreads rapidly in badly ventilated sites, at beginning of growing season and in late summer and early autumn. Cut the infected parts off as soon as seen; make sure plants have sufficient soil moisture and improve spacing of plants, branches or shoots. Spray benomyl, dinocap or a sulphur-containing fungicide.

Rust: fungus disease; raised brown-red spots, later turning black, on undersides of lower and older leaves, from late spring to late summer, mostly late in the summer. Collect and destroy infected leaves, as spores can overwinter on them; spray plants with a protective spray such as thiram or zineb, at two- to three-week intervals.

Shrubs, trees and fruit

Apple and pear canker: fungus disease; bark cracks, swells and flakes off. If branch or shoot encircled, it dies above canker. Disease enters through injuries, is worst in humid conditions and wet soil. Pare off diseased area back to healthy wood and paint wound with sealing compound or grafting wax. If too large, cut off affected part to below infection and treat cut area as above.

Apple codling moth: insect; pinkish grub feeds on pips and centre of apple from middle of early summer to end of mid-summer. Attacked apples may turn reddish, fall prematurely; collect and destroy. Apply sacking or corrugated cardboard bands to tree trunks late in mid-summer. Spray derris in the middle of early summer and again three weeks later if a bad attack is suspected. Repeat in late summer for second generation.

Apple (and plum) sawfly: insect; caterpillar which is dirty white with brown head, feeds on the flesh of young apples in late spring and early summer. Long, ribbon-like, corky scars on apple skin are also sawfly damage. Destroy infested fruits; spray g-HCH (BHC) at 80 per cent petal fall stage in bad infestations.

Apple and pear scab: fungus disease; infects leaves from early spring to mid-summer and is particularly bad in warm, rainy seasons. Black spots on leaves, brown markings down central vein of leaf and black spots on fruits, which later crack and rot. Infected young shoots have blistered bark, in which spores over-winter, for one year on apples and up to five years on pears. Cut off all such shoots when pruning in winter and destroy; collect and burn all fallen infected leaves and fruits during season and in autumn and spray with captan, benomyl, or sulphur-containing fungicide as in spray guide (see Mid-Winter).

Armillaria mellea *see* Honey fungus.

Azalea gall: fungus disease: young leaves thickened and twisted, with grey-white bloom on upper surface, and plants can be killed. Evergreen azaleas only are attacked. Pick off leaves and destroy; spray remainder with zineb to maintain protection.

Cherry (plum, peach) bacterial canker: bacterial disease; leaves in late spring have small round brown spots, which drop out, leaving 'shotholes'. Bark cracks and flakes off, may girdle shoot, branch or main trunk, all of which subsequently die. Leaves on such branches are pale green or yellow. Canker infection occurs in autumn through injuries. Obtain trees with resistant rootstocks; spray Bordeaux mixture at leaf-fall in autumn, again just before blossom opens and at petal fall. Remove unhealthy parts, treat wounds and do any pruning in spring or in summer immediately after picking.

Capsid bug: insect pest; distorts apple fruitlets badly as well as feeding on leaves. Control difficult without resorting to phosphorus insecticide such as dimethoate, but this may lead to build-up in red spider mite. Rely on predators if possible.

Clematis wilt: fungus disease; shoots of young plants wilt and collapse rapidly and suddenly. Cut off, to healthy growth, back to soil level if necessary, paint all cuts with sealing compound and spray subsequent growth with copper fungicide.

Fire blight: bacterial disease infecting shrubs and trees belonging to the rose family; flowers and leaves at tips of shoots turn black in spring, oozing patches appear just below bark; later, leaves wither and shoots appear to be burnt. Disease spreads rapidly in wet seasons and trees can be killed. No effective chemical control; cut out unhealthy shoots as soon as seen and destroy.

Holly leaf miner: insect; leaves have pale tunnels and blisters on surface, eventually wither and fall in bad attacks. Maggots feed within leaf tissue. Pick off and destroy infested leaves, spray remainder with dimethoate.

Apple blossom which has been caught by frost will have blackened centres and stamens. Such blossom will never set fruit and an entire crop may be destroyed.

The caterpillars of the lackey moth feed on the leaves of fruit trees and can cause severe defoliation.

Honey fungus: fungus disease; infects roots of woody plants. Toadstools with honey-coloured surface appear at base of affected plant, bark peels off to show white covering on wood beneath; spreads by means of black threads or 'bootlaces' in soil. Affected plants stop developing, leaves wilt and shoots and branches die. Burn dead plants, including roots; do not replant in same site. Treat roots of still living specimens and soil with creosote-based fungicide specific to honey fungus.

Mildew *see* Roses.

Peach-leaf curl (apricot, nectarine): fungus disease; spores over-winter beneath scales on outside of buds, infect leaves as they unfold in late winter and cause thickened, yellowish, later pink-to-red, distorted patches on leaves. Grey bloom on surface of patches in summer is spore-bearing stage which further infects leaves. Defoliation occurs, shoot growth stops and trees can be killed. Spray as buds open with copper or sulphur fungicide, repeat two weeks later and again in autumn, just as leaves start to fall. Destroy affected leaves as soon as seen and cut shoots back to healthy wood.

Pear-leaf blister mite: mite; in spring leaves have small, yellowish blisters which turn reddish and then black, fall prematurely. Fruitlets affected similarly. Hand-removal of affected parts is usually sufficient, otherwise spray lime-sulphur at bud burst stage.

Pear midge: insect; fruitlets deformed and enlarged, with central black cavity, in which will be one or more white maggots. Such fruitlets crack and fall prematurely. Hand-removal is usually sufficient, but in bad infestations, spraying with fenitrothion can be tried, remembering the possibility of red spider mite build up in consequence. Maggots may hibernate in soil two winters in succession.

Peony blight: fungus disease; new young shoots and young flower buds wilt suddenly; buds lower down on the stem turn brown and brown patches, later coated with grey mould, may appear on older leaves. Spray thiram or captan as leaves appear in spring and repeat at two-week intervals until flowering. Cut off all affected parts to healthy growth and paint cut surfaces with sealing compound.

Red plum maggot: insect; red caterpillar feeds in centre of fruits from early summer to early autumn and then hibernates in suitable hiding place until following spring. Treat as for apple codling moth.

Rhododendron bud blast: fungus disease; buds turn brown or grey-brown from autumn onward and by winter have growth of black bristles on them. Buds are killed; frost-damaged buds do not have black bristles. Remove infected buds and a little stem and destroy. Control leaf-hoppers, by spraying in mid-summer with derris or malathion, as they indirectly help to ensure the spread of the disease.

Silver leaf: fungus disease; infects plum, cherry; apple, pear, peach, nectarine and apricot to a lesser extent, also shrubs, especially laburnum and laurel. Leaves silvered on one complete shoot or branch, wood stained brown internally. When tree or shrub killed, purple and yellowish brown, plate-like growths appear from the branches. In advanced attacks, infected branches of tree should be removed and burnt and wounds covered with sealing compound. Improved feeding and manuring should enable remainder to recover. Prune when infection unlikely, from early to late summer.

Vine and clay-coloured weevil: insect; adult beetles, small and black or brown, eat holes in margins of rhododendron, rose and vine leaves. White grubs feed on roots of various shrubs and vines. Fork HCH (BHC) dust into soil occasionally from mid-summer to late winter, to deal with the grubs, and dust leaves lightly from early spring to early autumn, for adult control.

Woolly aphis (American blight): insect; patches of white cotton-wool appear on bark of apple trees, especially at junctions of shoots and branches. Does little direct harm, but looks unsightly, makes picking messy and provides entry for disease through injury made by feeding. Brush away with stiff brush, paint patches with methylated spirits or spray forcibly with derris, from early summer, as necessary.